LAS MOCEDADES DE RODRIGO
THE YOUTHFUL DEEDS OF RODRIGO, THE CID

Perhaps the most famous Castilian in history, Rodrigo Diaz – also known as 'the Cid' – lived in the second half of the eleventh century and distinguished himself during the conquest of the Muslim kingdom of Valencia. The epic poem *Las Mocedades de Rodrigo* (*The Youthful Deeds of Rodrigo*) is a fictional account of the young Rodrigo's passage from impetuous initiate to menacing force of nature, and, finally, to ally and servitor of his king. Written around 1300, the poem garnered a significant reputation in its native Spain and is still widely read today. Despite its popularity, an English translation has never been published.

This bilingual edition offers both the Old Spanish version of *Las Mocedades* as well as the first English translation of the epic poem. In his introduction, Matthew Bailey examines the text as a compilation of oral narratives passed down from speakers to scribes. Situating it fully within the tradition of Spanish epic poetry, Bailey goes on to review the poem's critical reception, explains the hybrid nature of the narrative, and looks at the origins of the hero himself. The translation includes explanatory notes to help the contemporary English-language reader understand the social and political circumstances surrounding the poem. For those interested in the poetry of medieval Spain, the epic tradition, or for anyone looking for a good adventure story, *Las Mocedades de Rodrigo* will be essential reading.

MATTHEW BAILEY is a professor in the Department of Romance Languages at Washington and Lee University.

Medieval Academy Books, No. 110

Las Mocedades de Rodrigo

The Youthful Deeds of Rodrigo, the Cid

Edited and translated by Matthew Bailey

Published for the Medieval Academy of America by
University of Toronto Press

University of Toronto Press
Toronto Buffalo London
Printed in the U.S.A.

Reprinted in paperback 2013

ISBN 978-0-8020-9336-3 (cloth)
ISBN 978-1-4426-1595-3 (paper)

Printed on acid-free paper

Library and Archives Canada Cataloguing in Publication

Las mocedades de Rodrigo = The youthful deeds of Rodrigo,
the Cid / edited and translated by Matthew Bailey.

(Medieval academy books; 110)
Includes the original text in old Spanish.
ISBN 978-0-8020-9336-3 (bound). – ISBN 978-1-4426-1595-3 (pbk.)

1. Cid, ca. 1043–1099 – Poetry.   2. Mocedades de Rodrigo.
I. Bailey, Matthew   II. Medieval Academy of America
III. Title: Youthful deeds of Rodrigo, the Cid.   IV. Series.

PQ6366.A4 2007   861'.1   C2007-901897-1

University of Toronto Press acknowledges the financial assistance to
its publishing program of the Canada Council for the Arts
and the Ontario Arts Council.

Canada Council   Conseil des Arts
for the Arts   du Canada

ONTARIO ARTS COUNCIL
CONSEIL DES ARTS DE L'ONTARIO
50 YEARS OF ONTARIO GOVERNMENT SUPPORT OF THE ARTS
50 ANS DE SOUTIEN DU GOUVERNEMENT DE L'ONTARIO AUX ARTS

University of Toronto Press acknowledges the financial support for
its publishing activities of the Government of Canada through
the Book Publishing Industry Development Program (BPIDP).

For Nina Clara and Ana Camila, mis infantas

CONTENTS

ACKNOWLEDGMENTS

I would like to recognize two people who have contributed immeasurably to the completion of this volume, from its early inception to its present fruition. I am most grateful to my good friend and mentor Thomas Montgomery for his insightful comments on my initial translation of the poem, and for his generosity in sharing with me his expertise on this poem and the epic genre in general. For many years now his writings and reflections have illuminated my understanding of epic poetry and inspired me to probe further. I will remain forever in the debt of my wife and partner, Cristina Ferreira-Pinto Bailey, who urged me to envision an audience of readers with a curiosity equal to mine, and who might also understand that the poem's imperfections are its strength and the source of its brilliance.

I also wish to recognize and thank Richard K. Emmerson, former executive director of the Medieval Academy of America, who was instrumental in navigating the volume through the occasionally rough waters of Hispano-medievalism to its current safe harbour. I thank him for his goodwill and patience, and for his persistence in the review process. I am grateful as well for the comments of the anonymous reviewers who may take satisfaction in seeing their suggestions reflected in the text.

LAS MOCEDADES DE RODRIGO

INTRODUCTION

Spain produced a rich store of epic narratives presented orally before eager audiences for centuries. Yet most of the evidence is found in prose chronicles and not in verse manuscripts. The earliest example is a brief passage in Latin detailing some of the protagonists of an epic tale that would appear later in manuscript form as the *Chanson de Roland*. Known to scholars as the *Nota Emilianense*, the passage dates from 1075 and is an early indicator of the popularity of epic narratives in northern Spain (Alonso 1954, 9). Carolingian themes continue to appear prominently in historical chronicles and ballads well into the Renaissance, but only the *Cantar de Roncesvalles* – a passage of 100 lines contained on two folios from the late thirteenth century – preserves verses from the medieval period. Thirteenth-century prose histories of Christian Spain incorporate into their narratives the epic deeds of the warrior class, at first in Latin with some trepidation, but when the Castilian vernacular assumes its role as the official language of León-Castile in the latter half of the thirteenth century, the epic tales suddenly exhibit the rich characterization and compelling plots of a thriving literary tradition. When the chroniclers note discrepancies between the Latin accounts and contemporary oral sources, they identify minstrels, or *juglares*, as the purveyors of the oral narratives (Menéndez Pidal 1924, 366–70). The chroniclers acknowledge a bias for the historical accuracy of the venerable written accounts, but they cannot resist incorporating the more lively oral narratives into their histories (Fradejas Lebrero 1991, esp. 36–8).

The chroniclers were engaged in producing the first full-scale vernacular history of Spain under the direction of Alfonso X, king of León-Castile from 1252 to 1284. The completed project, known to scholars today as the *Estoria de España*, is a convincing testimony to the prominence of oral epic in medieval Spain. The epic tales begin to take centre stage in the chapters covering the tenth and the eleventh centuries, when the two principal Castilian epic heroes emerge, Fernán González and Rodrigo Díaz de Vivar, el Cid. Other epics are included in the Alfonsine history, the most compelling of which are tragic in nature, such as *Siete infantes de Lara*, *Bernardo del Carpio*, and *Sancho II*, but Fernán González and Rodrigo Díaz enjoy pride of place as the most successful and fiercely independent of the Castilian warriors.

Fernán González was actively engaged in war and politics in the second quarter of the tenth century, gaining considerable independence for the county of Castile from the kingdoms of León and Navarre in 945 AD. He was astute politically, but his real source of status was his ability to turn back the incessant raids of the Muslims to the south. In the prose and verse narratives that recount his deeds, he is known as the liberator of Castile. The most complete poem of his deeds is an epic tale recast as a learned narrative, the *Poema de Fernán González* (here *Fernán González*), which portrays him as the first independent count of Castile. The Alfonsine chroniclers included the tale in their prose history, but they rejected his celebrated challenge to royal authority by recasting his confrontation with the king of León as dutiful submission (Bailey 1996).

Rodrigo Díaz lived in the second half of the eleventh century (ca. 1045–99) and is surely the most celebrated Castilian in history. During his lifetime a Latin panegyric poem of some 129 lines, the *Carmen Campidoctoris*, enthusiastically celebrates Rodrigo's exploits in the field of battle. This anonymous poem begins by relating his background and his service in the royal households of Sancho II of Castile and Alfonso VI of León-Castile. It recounts his youthful triumph over a champion from Navarre, his victory over an army led by the Castilian Count García Ordóñez, and the preparations for his victorious battle over the Count of Barcelona at Almenar. The battle is never recounted, since the final lines of the poem were erased from the manuscript. The *Carmen* has been dated to 1083, some ten years prior to Rodrigo's conquest of the Muslim kingdom of Valencia in 1094, his greatest feat (Fletcher 1989, 92–3).

An untitled biography of Rodrigo's life was put to parchment in Latin prose not long after his death, an anonymous prose text known as the *Historia Roderici*. It provides a fairly detailed account of the events leading up to Rodrigo's exile from Castile in 1081, his service to the Muslim king of Zaragoza, and his return to Castile in 1086. Even more attention is given to the narration of the raids and battles that led to the eventual conquest of Valencia in 1094. But the *Historia Roderici* also mentions a few episodes from Rodrigo's youth, such as the victorious single combat against the champion from Navarre, and Rodrigo's marriage to Jimena as a reward for service to the royal household of Alfonso VI.

Although Fernán González was surely celebrated in epic verse before Rodrigo Díaz, those earlier compositions were lost or simply never put to parchment. There are only two full-length Spanish poems preserved in the traditional epic verse associated with the oral tradition of minstrels, and both of them recreate the life of Rodrigo Díaz. The best known is the *Cantar de Mio Cid*, or *Poem of Mio Cid*, here *Mio Cid*. It is a classic text of world literature that celebrates the mature hero, *Mio Cid*, 'My Lord,' beginning with his exile from Castile and ending with his death in 1099, at the height of the fame and honour he won for himself and his family through the conquest of the Muslim kingdom of Valencia. The *Mocedades de Rodrigo* or *Youthful Deeds of Rodrigo*, here *Mocedades*, is a work familiar mostly to Hispano-medievalists. The poem tells the fictional story of the passage of a precocious twelve-year-old Rodrigo from a rebellious and destructive killing force of nature to a leader of men in the service of his king, Fernando I of León-Castile (1035–60).

THE *MOCEDADES* MANUSCRIPT: DATE AND PROVENANCE

The *Mocedades* occupies the final folios (ff. 188–201) of a paper manuscript housed in the Bibliothèque Nationale in Paris, France (ms. Fonds espagnol, 12). Folios 1–187 of the manuscript contain one of numerous versions of the *Crónica de los reyes de Castilla (Crónica de Castilla)*. Its main focus is on the reigns of King Fernando I and his two sons, King Sancho II of Castile and King Alfonso VI of León. These are the kings who reigned during the lifetime of Rodrigo, and this chronicle shows a special affinity for tales involving the Castilian warrior hero. It draws much of its material from Alfonso's *Estoria de España*, but is distinct enough in tenor to be considered post-Alfonsine. The same hand copied the chronicle and the poem, and on the final folio of the manuscript (f. 201), the year 1400 AD is etched, although ink was never applied. The date seems not to be written in the same hand as the remainder of the manuscript, so its reliability as an indicator of the date the manuscript was penned is not entirely clear (Funes 2004, xxviiin13).

In 1844 the *Mocedades* manuscript was brought to the attention of modern scholars by Eugenio de Ochoa. In the first bibliographical notice of the poem, Ochoa describes its initial folios as an assemblage of unequal fragments from different authors and periods, part chronicle and part poorly rhymed verse, its language uneven with so little connection between passages (*períodos*) that it frequently becomes unintelligible (paraphrase of Ochoa 1844, 110). Ramón Menéndez Pidal, Spain's pre-eminent medievalist of the twentieth century, acknowledged the patchwork nature of the narrative, especially in its description of early Castilian history prior to the appearance of Rodrigo in the narrative. Yet he also recognized in it the emergence of a new heroic model, an audacious youth who acts impetuously in challenging his father, his king, and other figures of authority who attempt to diminish his fierce sense of clannish pride and independence (Menéndez Pidal 1924, 406).

This impetuous youth is the same Rodrigo who would figure prominently in later Spanish literature, especially in the ballads and dramatic works of the sixteenth and seventeenth centuries. Menéndez Pidal was the first scholar to discern the underlying coherence or artistic unity of the *Mocedades* in its linking of the early history of Castile, which he terms a prologue, with the narrative of Rodrigo's youthful deeds. He surmised that the entire narrative was composed in writing by a minstrel, or *juglar*, intent on showing off his extensive knowledge of the early Castilian rulers and history (Menéndez Pidal 1924, 406). Yet much of this historical prologue was in blatant contradiction to prose and verse narratives that the minstrel must have known, and therefore purposefully outlandish and contrived in an attempt to garner the attention of his audience (410–11). Menéndez Pidal also emphasized that other epic narratives had similar introductory material and suggested that the learned *Fernán González*, with a similar prologue, served as the model for the composition of the *Mocedades* (407–8). Also noted was the prominence of the history of the diocese of Palencia in the narrative, which led Menéndez Pidal to propose that it was written by a minstrel from Palencia sometime between the end of the fourteenth and the beginning of the fifteenth centuries (406).

Subsequent efforts to date the *Mocedades* have involved comparisons to the *Crónica de Castilla*, the first chronicle to narrate episodes from Rodrigo's youth in detail. It was most likely composed between 1290 and 1300, a date based on its translation into Galician between 1295 and 1312 (Armistead 2000, 39–40). Since the approximate date of the chronicle is widely acknowledged, and that of the *Mocedades* is unclear, episodes from both have been scrutinized in an attempt to clarify their relationship (Armistead 1955, 117–58). The comparison of chronicle and poem shows that the episodes of Rodrigo's youth are similar enough in structure to conclude that a version of the *Mocedades* narrative was employed in the composition of the *Crónica de Castilla*. Although not necessarily the same narrative as the one preserved in the extant manuscript, a narrative quite similar to the *Mocedades* must have emerged between 1289, the end of the Alfonsine historiography that tells little of Rodrigo's youth, and 1300, the date assigned to completion of the *Crónica de Castilla* (1312 for Martin 1992, 435, 470).

The oral narrative poem that was incorporated into the *Crónica de Castilla* circa 1300 is similar in much of its basic plot structure to the story of Rodrigo's youth told in the *Mocedades*. There are some important differences between the two stories, however. The most significant may be the insertion of a fairly extensive narrative on the foundation and subsequent trials of the diocese of Palencia into the textual fabric of the *Mocedades*. Alan Deyermond rightly noted the peculiarity of this ecclesiastical foundation legend in the midst of an otherwise epic text. On the basis of his substantial research into the history of the diocese, Deyermond identified a period of crisis in Palencia that may have served to embolden a secular cleric to compose the *Mocedades* text in order to link the political claims of his diocese to the heroic history of Castile. His written composition adapted a traditional oral epic poem on the young Rodrigo Díaz to suit his propagandistic ends (1969, 198; reaffirmed in 1999, 14–15). Perhaps the most innovative aspect of Deyermond's approach was his research on the early history of the diocese of Palencia, and the identification of the civil wars between Pedro I (1350–69) of León-Castile and his half-brother Enrique II de Trastámara as the catalyst for the composition of the poem. Deyermond suggests that the episode of the invasion of France by Rodrigo in the *Mocedades* may indicate support on the part of the Palencia cleric for Pedro I against his half-brother Enrique, who was allied in his quest for the throne with Aragon and France, a coalition supported by the pope (Deyermond 1969, 196). Since Pedro was murdered by Enrique in 1369, the poem was likely composed prior to that date, and most likely not after 1366, when Enrique overran the north and had himself proclaimed king (1969, 197).

Georges Martin, following Deyermond's lead in privileging historical factors in pinpointing a date of composition for the *Mocedades*, concluded that the manuscript text was produced just prior to 1325 (1992, 471). Martin brushes aside Deyermond's later date by singling out the portrayal of Rodrigo as a rebellious and defiant youth in the *Mocedades* and linking his behaviour to the unfortunate minorities of Fernando IV (1295–1312) and Alfonso XI (1312–25). In Martin's formulation, Rodrigo's rebelliousness is seen as a literary response to the historical incompetence of these child kings, reminiscent of the portrayal of the child king Fernando I in the *Mocedades*. Both Deyermond and Martin understand the text as a single composition, the work of an individual author who took a traditional epic narrative as the basis for his composition.

Leonardo Funes argues for a more nuanced compositional process that envisions three distinct stages leading to the extant manuscript text. The first stage, or *estado*, is the transcription of the traditional epic narrative, the *Gesta*, just prior to 1300. The second stage, a rewriting, or *Refundición*, is carried out by a cleric associated with the diocese of Palencia around 1300. This cleric added to the *Gesta* narrative material associated with his home diocese. The third stage produced the *Crónica rimada*, or rhymed chronicle, the extant manuscript text of 1400, which was copied from the hypothetical *Refundición* with little regard for its poetic features, but with a notable interest in adding genealogies and honorifics related to the protagonists of the poem (Funes 2004, xxix–xxxix).

The concept of three stages of redaction may not be agreeable to all specialists, but it is a reasonable accounting of a manuscript bearing signs of multiple written modifications that scholars have acknowledged for some time (Montgomery 1984a, esp. 12). The most noteworthy modifications to the text are the three episodes relating to the foundation and struggle for survival of the diocese of Palencia. This material is not epic in nature, nor is it directly related to Rodrigo either historically or mythically. Funes follows Deyermond in sugesting that the Palenica material was added to the *Mocedades* narrative in an attempt to link the diocese to the heroic warriors of Castile, and most especially to the growing popularity of Rodrigo (Funes 2004, xxxiv).

Later interventions take the form of lengthened lines in which names have been expanded, titles added, and genealogical information provided. These reflect a kind of precision and attention to detail associated with the fourteenth-century Portuguese *Livro de linhagens*, a courtly chronicle far removed from the focus on heroic deeds characteristic of epic narrative (Funes 2004, xxxii–xxxiii). For Funes, the nature of these later interventions reveals the presence of a third hand recopying a pre-existing manuscript text, with the likely intention of heightening its documentary credibility, as noted by Thomas Montgomery (1984a, esp. 4–5). Although the Palencia additions were made in verse form, the genealogical and titular interventions display little regard for verse, especially evident in the insertion of the Laínez genealogies (ll. 300–13).

The same hand copied the text of the *Mocedades* and the *Crónica de Castilla* onto the extant manuscript. It is plainly legible, somewhat attractive in its rendering of a few oversized capital letters, although otherwise without adornment. It has been reproduced in photographic facsimile twice, first in black and white (Huntington 1904), and more recently in colour (Bailey, ed., 1999, included between pages 182 and 183). On each folio of the manuscript the text is presented in two columns, which works well enough for the prose chronicle but is entirely inappropriate for verse, leading to the disruption of verses and the loss of some end-line assonance. The text of the *Mocedades* is also marred by occasional lacunae that, in addition to the interpolations, disrupt the flow of the narrative and an otherwise compelling tale.

THE *MOCEDADES* STORY

While we await a final verdict on the question of the date and provenance of the extant *Mocedades* manuscript, we might well note that its late discovery serves as a reminder that the medieval chronicles, the later folk ballads, Guillén de Castro's Golden Age drama *Las mocedades del Cid*, Pierre Corneille's *Le Cid*, and Robert Southey's *Chronicle of the Cid*, all retold a similar story of Rodrigo's youth with no knowledge of the extant copy of the *Mocedades*. Because medieval narratives were oral in their genesis and transmission, narrators were not so much authors as mediators between the narratives and their audiences. The audience response contributed to shaping the narrative as it was delivered. If any part of a performance was unappealing, inappropriate, or otherwise objectionable, an audience's negative response would compel the narrator to modify the story. A positive response might encourage the narrator to offer more details or to narrate an additional episode similar in tenor, perhaps even borrowing from other stories. This synergy between audience and narrator is why the medieval narratives are ideal testimonies to the values, hopes, and fears of the communities that nourished them. They have stood the test of multiple audiences through countless performances and are, by virtue of their oral dissemination, classic works.

In its basic outline, the story of Rodrigo's youth is richly suggestive. The hero is the descendant of legendary warrior lords who governed Castile in times of constant aggression. The heroine is the daughter of a count killed in retaliatory combat by the young hero. Their marriage is imposed on the hero in order to appease the need for vengeance in a recent blood feud, and to save the king from disturbing the uneasy alliance between the Castilian and Leonese factions of his kingdom. But the story is also about the initiation of a young man into adulthood, and the role of a woman in that process. Jimena demands Rodrigo's hand in marriage and in doing so makes him part of a community larger than his extended family and alliances. Her intrusion into Rodrigo's world forces him to look beyond family ties for a productive role for himself, eventually leading him to the service of his king. Initially he is full of bravura, but this posture masks insecurities about his social stature and the fear that he may not measure up to the king and the counts of the court. Rodrigo must face up to these insecurities and transcend the ties of his youth in order to become the king's most trusted warrior in the service of his country. The ending of the poem is missing from the manuscript, but from other sources we may presume that Rodrigo would return to his homeland in triumph, marry the woman who compelled him to think on a grand scale, and go on to fulfil his destiny as the most celebrated warrior in the history of Spain (Hook and Long 1999, 66–7).

Even this brief review of the plot reveals a compelling story with mythic resonances that transcend the particular deeds of Rodrigo's youth. Rodrigo's first killing at the age of twelve recalls the myth of warrior initiation, which has an identifiable prototype in the chief Irish epic hero Cúchulainn, from the great saga *Táin Bó Cúailnge* (Montgomery 1998, 11). Elements of this myth were widespread in ancient and medieval Europe and, although they are present to some degree in all the Spanish epic narratives, they are most prominent in the *Mocedades* (Montgomery 1998, 29–41; 1999). Like Cúchulainn, Rodrigo is a child hero who kills, his uncontrollable rage produces physical transformations and makes him invincible, his warrior prowess is a menace to his own society, and his destructive urges are finally subdued by a confrontation with the feminine. Rodrigo's betrothal to Jimena sets him on the path to integration into society, a process that begins with his defiant vow to win five pitched battles before consummating his marriage. His quest culminates in an expedition undertaken with King Fernando I that takes them to the very gates of Paris to answer the aggressions of the king of France. Later versions of the *Mocedades* story privilege one or another of the components of the tale. The popular folk ballads, the seventeenth-century play, and the Hollywood film *El Cid* all select elements from the plot and expand on them. In the case of the ballads, a folk tradition in which all segments of society participated as disseminators and as audience, the focus on Rodrigo's rebelliousness and on Jimena's distress at being orphaned should be seen as fairly transparent reflections of the hopes and fears of late-medieval Spanish society. In the *Mocedades del Cid*, authored by Guillén de Castro in 1612, the playwright incorporated some of the relevant ballads into his dramatic dialogue, but in his choice of plot he is guided more by the social norms and strictures of the time as well as by the genre of theatre and audience expectation. Rodrigo is no longer rebellious, and Jimena's distress is fuelled by the conflict between her passionate love for Rodrigo and her role as the dutiful daughter who must avenge her father's death. The Hollywood film *El Cid* incorporates many of the elements of the plot of the *Mocedades*, as well as others from the *Mio Cid* and the *Mocedades del Cid*, but the diverse elements are tweaked to attach them to a distinctly Hollywoodian hero who fights for God, Alfonso, and Spain (Jancovic 2000, 94–8).

As the variant versions of Rodrigo's life manifest, the most important quality of a hero is not conformity to strict historical fact, but adaptability to evolving conceptions of heroic behaviour. Rodrigo returned to life many times after his natural death because the story of his youth continued to be told in ways that allowed diverse audiences to see themselves in him. As the audiences changed, the story responded to new standards of behaviour and social conditions, to audience hopes and fears, even to nostalgia for the past, a phenomenon attested to throughout the Middle Ages (Eco 1986, 84).

Like these other versions of Rodrigo's youth, the manuscript text of the *Mocedades* also testifies to specific cultural and institutional interests. The transcription of the poem onto parchment could take place only after being authorized by an institution, probably at the behest of the clerics of Palencia who would have their own reasons for wanting a written copy of a popular oral narrative they knew well. In order to better understand how this process might have worked in the case of the *Mocedades*, we should begin by looking more closely at other examples of the utilization of oral narratives in the construction of historical realities.

THE COMPOSITION OF THE *MOCEDADES*

In the *Historia Roderici*, the narrator tells us that he is moved to write by a desire to rescue the deeds of Rodrigo from oblivion. This may be best understood as a response to the oral dissemination of a Cid narrative and perhaps to an unfavourable portrayal of its protagonist (Barton and Fletcher 2000, 96). A close reading of the text suggests that three aspects of the Cid's legacy are in play: his loyalty to Alfonso, his cruelty towards his enemies, and his merit as a warrior. The *Mio Cid* was most likely written down by the monks at the monastery of San Pedro de Cardeña, the Cid's original burial site, to be used as an authoritative text to satisfy the devotees of their prosperous tomb cult (Russell 1958, 79; Fletcher 1989, 195–200; Bailey 2003, 266–7). The clerical influences evident in the *Fernán González* point to a substantive link between the Castilian monastery of San Pedro de Arlanza and the count who helped sustain it (Salvador Martínez 1991, 10, 28–35).

The import of epic narratives may be best understood through their abundant representation in the recreations of the recent past by the thirteenth-century chroniclers in the employ of Alfonso X. These medieval historians expressly acknowledged the oral transmission of the heroic narratives they appropriated (Menéndez-Pidal 1924, 366–70), and while they questioned the veracity of the vernacular tales when they clashed with the written – that is, Latin versions of the same stories – they did not refrain from incorporating them wholesale into the chronicles. But the Alfonsine historians incorporated these vernacular tales after manipulating their content to support Alfonso's political agenda of presenting himself as the natural ruler of all Spain, and to provide instruction on the respect due a natural lord, vicar of God on Earth, through the exercise of reason (English paraphrase of Fernández-Ordóñez 2000, 43). Writing was also an expensive and time-consuming proposition, and while scribes were engaged in preserving narrations of the lives of kings, they were most often employed in documenting the exchange of property and other kinds of legal or mercantile activity. The putting to parchment of an oral narrative required justification of its expense and, more importantly, a reason for superseding its continuing dissemination by minstrels. The preservation on parchment of the *Mocedades* clearly represents exceptional treatment for a vernacular narrative in Spain, and it compels us to ask why a monastery or other powerful institution would engage the valuable resources of its scriptorium in its placement on parchment, especially one of Rodrigo Díaz, a venerated warrior to be sure, but no king.

The clerics of Palencia must have been familiar with the story of Rodrigo's youth that was circulating orally at the time. Its authority had to be beyond dispute in order for them to believe that it would constitute a coherent message in support of the diocese (Deyermond 1999, 12). By linking Rodrigo's *mocedades* and other narratives of the legendary warriors of Castile to the foundation of the Palencia diocese, its transformation into a bishopric, its survival through harrowing times, and its extensive land claims, the clerics hoped the diocese would gain prestige. This is a reasonable explanation for the production of the written text, since no minstrel could have imagined, much less produced, such a hybrid text (Montgomery 1984a, 12–14). But the poem is composed in such a piecemeal fashion that a clear ideological message has proven difficult to discern, even for modern readers who enjoy the luxury of reflection and multiple readings of the written text (Funes 2004, lix–lx). A medieval audience, after hearing the poem performed orally, would be unlikely to understand it as an unequivocal call for support of the diocese.

The *Mocedades* narrative does have one overarching theme that binds all its disparate elements togther, that links the Palencia material and the lives of the legendary warriors of Castile, and that may explain the writing of the poem. Every episode of the poem is imbued with the protagonist's determination to fight for independence and self-rule. This is most evident in the fierce independence of the protagonists from the Castilian warrior class, but is also shared by the Palencia bishops who defend their shrine and later bishopric against all aggressors. Rodrigo's exploits are the most detailed and occupy roughly three-quarters of the narrative, but his independent impulses and his overwhelming ferocity in battle are presaged in the narration of the deeds of his ancestors. The composition is uneven, poorly developed in many regards, and frustratingly sparse in the kind of detail and nuance that characterize the *Mio Cid.* It gives the impression of having been composed from passages of disparate narratives crudely joined together, but this hybrid composition communicates a genealogy of Castilians unanimously determined to settle for nothing less than independence for themselves and their people, and fully capable of defending their aspirations on the field of battle or at court.

Within this narrative of the history of Castilian warriors struggling for independence, the diocese of Palencia is portrayed in a parallel fashion, with details of its humble beginnings, its conversion into a bishopric, and its struggles to preserve its status and independence. In the first instance, the Palencia material includes a description of the discovery of an ancient shrine to Saint Antolín Martyr, already some three hundred years old when it was discovered by Bernardo, a knight of King Sancho III Garcés (1000–35). King Sancho then receives the shrine from Count Pedro of Palencia in exchange for Campó, and its guardianship is conferred on Bernardo. The second passage relates the transfer of the bishopric from Toledo, overrun by Muslims, to Palencia in the person of Bishop Miro, Bernardo's uncle. A charter signed by King Sancho and confirmed by the pope identifies the lands granted to the bishopric, and King Sancho finalizes its approval with a curse on any son of his who dares transgress its privileges. The third passage relates the death of Bishop Miro, the transfer of the bishopric to Bernardo, reconfirmation of the charter by the pope, and by the son of the deceased King Sancho, King Fernando I, and the identification of the lands included in the charter. A final passage narrates the expulsion of Bishop Bernardo from the bishopric by the sons of Count Pedro of Palencia, and Bernardo's plea for assistance to King Fernando, who can only lament Rodrigo's absence, which has left him incapable of resolving the dispute. The bishop then expresses his determination to journey to Rome for a resolution.

Through this narrative the Palencia diocese reaffirms its legitimacy and its rights by royal charter. It also establishes a bond with the most revered ancestors of the Castilian nobility, invoking key links in their common history and a like-minded willingness to fight any aggression designed to deprive them of their ancestral right to independence. Scholars have not seen the Palencia material as establishing a parallel between the struggles of the early defenders and advocates of the Palencia shrine and the early Castilians who won the right to govern themselves by facing down their aggressors. While the propagation of a clear political message in support of the diocese of Palencia seems to be an unlikely outcome of this jumbled narrative, the parallels indicated here are clearly communicated and could have been quite successful in encouraging the clerics and their supporters to fight their aggressors and to free themselves from the depredations of their enemies.

Epic poetry typically features one hero, with most of the attention focused on recounting his deeds. This is the case in the *Mio Cid*, the *Chanson de Roland, Beowulf*, and other medieval heroic narratives. The *Mocedades* breaks this mould by narrating the deeds of earlier Castilian heroes such as Fernán González, King Sancho Garcés, and the mature King Fernando I before turning to the deeds of the twelve-year-old Rodrigo and the adolescent King Fernando I. What these early Castilians, including the mature King Fernando, have in common with Rodrigo is their unwavering commitment to independence. In

the narration of his deeds, Rodrigo is abruptly introduced to the Leonese court
of the adolescent King Fernando and through his actions and counsel eventu-
ally helps the king stand tall against the enemies of his kingdom. Unlike other
epic poems, the *Mocedades* does not focus exclusively on one hero, but instead
plots a genealogy of heroic Castilians driven by a desire for independence and
equipped with the tenacity to fight for it.

Understood in this way, the poem has thematic unity and the Palencia story
fits well within it. The protagonists are clerics, not warriors, but the defence of
their privileges is just as tenacious as Rodrigo's battles against his enemies.
The thematic unity of the poem is an abstraction, of course. Its conception of a
common history linking diverse protagonists is at odds with the individualistic
attitude of Rodrigo and the mythic essence of heroism. The compositional
process involved an ability to look beyond the tales of heroic deeds by recog-
nizing in them a common thread, and linking them to the trials of the early
clerics of Palencia. The intellectual basis for this composition is a vision of
history in which individual deeds are incorporated into a broader and more
abstract conception that imbues them with meaning. The impulse is learned,
literate in its essence, and in the medieval period is solely attributable to a
cleric. Since the composition reaffirms the foundational claims and the contin-
ued legitimacy of the bishopric of Palencia, it stands to reason that the cleric
would be closely associated with that institution, as first noted by Deyermond
(1969, 81; 1999, 12).

This is not to suggest that one or more clerics from Palencia authored the
poem in the modern sense of writing an original story, but that they did orga-
nize an overall theme reinforced through a series of episodes from pre-existing
narratives. These heroic tales were circulating orally at the time, and their
theme of defiance must have inspired the Palencia clerics to compose a narra-
tive of their own, as a means to reinforce their determination to defend their
claim to the lands they held and their ecclesiastical status as a bishopric. They
later integrated their story into a somewhat contrived narrative of Castilian
independence in a way that emphasized a historic struggle for independent
rule and a common defence against all aggressors.

THE *MOCEDADES* NARRATIVE

Castilian epic narratives demonstrate a preference for recreating the struggles
of strong-willed nobles, sometimes referred to as rebel or defiant vassals
(Vaquero 1999, 102; 2005, 221). This tendency is evidenced in the epic tales
preserved in prose prior to the composition of the *Mocedades*, and is even more
pronounced in the popular ballads that first began to appear in print toward the

end of the sixteenth century. In both epic and ballad Castilian nobles are portrayed as aggressive defenders of their birthright to self-governance. This is also the main theme of the *Mocedades* narrative, beginning with the Castilian ancestors of Rodrigo and King Fernando, Laín Calvo, and Nuño Rasura respectively, who are subjects of the king of León but are also responsible for the defence of Castile. Fernán González, a grandson of Nuño Rasura, wins Castile from the king of León, initially through defiant resistance to his rule, but ultimately as payment on an overdue debt. His great-grandson, Sancho, is proclaimed the first king of Castile. After inheriting the kingdom of León, Sancho neglects Castile, and the Castilians revolt. His son, Fernando I, inherits the kingdom of Castile and conquers the other Christian kingdoms of Spain, including León. He and his Castilian vassals convene and concur that his flag should bear the Castilian castle and the Leonese lion, thus acknowledging Castile and León as equals.

A feud between the Laínez clan of Castile (Rodrigo's father and uncles) and Count Gómez of Gormaz, Jimena's father, thrusts Rodrigo into the narrative and sets the stage for the initial confrontation between the young Rodrigo and the adolescent King Fernando. Rodrigo first refuses to recognize Fernando's authority, but as they confront domestic enemies and European powers determined to submit Spain to their authority, Rodrigo begins to recognize that the king's enemies are his own. Eventually they invade France together, taking their armies to the very gates of Paris.

Some of this material is familiar from earlier epics, such as the story of Fernán González, but much resurfaces also in later ballads (Montgomery 1984b). These defiant protagonists and their zeal for self-determination represent a popular attitude manifested in narratives over hundreds of years. The Palencia clerics, with their diocese under siege and suffering repeated challenges to its legal authority and physical integrity, also portray their predecessors as wilful defenders of their rights. In order to compose a narrative with a single thematic focus, the composer of the *Mocedades* selected only those passages from pre-existing narratives that recreated struggles for independence and the defiant attitudes that fuelled them. These selected narratives surely contained additional episodes unrelated to the fierce defence of self-governance, but these would have been of little interest and quickly cast aside. The result of this compositional process is an exclusive focus on the Castilian struggle for independence, although the *Mocedades* narrative also contains a number of incomplete passages, suffers from a lack of narrative flow, and offers little detail or nuance.

The composer of the *Mocedades* would have taken material from full-length epics, surely a biography of the young Rodrigo, and from shorter narratives, precursors to folk ballads or *romances* (Montgomery 1984b, 132). This process involved oral dictation by minstrels, scribes writing down the dictated texts on wax tablets, and the transfer of select passages from their original contexts to a new composition. Some additional writing was needed to blend the disparate sources, but judging from the sparse expression of the poem, rewriting was minimal. Variety of assonance especially seems to have been sacrificed, resulting in the use of the unremarkable *a-o* assonance in over 80 per cent of the verses in the *Mocedades*, in part by employing the same words repeatedly (133).

The Alfonsine chroniclers established a precedent for this compositional model when in the latter half of the thirteenth century they conceived and composed the *Estoria de España* in a similar fashion, with one important difference. Whereas in the *Mocedades* the emphasis is on highlighting a pedigree of Castilian defiance in the name of autonomy, the Alfonsine chroniclers laboured to expunge acts of rebelliousness from their narrative (Fernández-Ordóñez, ed., 1993, 182–3). In fact, the two most celebrated challenges to royal authority in the Spanish epic – the confrontation between Fernán González and King Alfonso of León, and the aggressive response of Rodrigo to the royal authority of King Fernando – were written out of the *Estoria de España* (Bailey 1999, 92–3) and the *Crónica de Castilla* respectively (Catalán 2000, 81, 87–8), only to come roaring back to life in the *Mocedades* and later ballads.

In this sense, the *Mocedades* represents an anti-Alfonsine composition, narrating heroic acts of defiance only recently censored in the writing of the official history of Spain. In both cases, however, oral narratives were recorded by dictation and later employed, often in a piecemeal fashion, in the writing of a more comprehensive and ideologically motivated history. The Alfonsine chroniclers began their compilations in 1270 and completed the project in stages, but seem to have been decommissioned by 1289, during the brief reign of Alfonso's son Sancho IV. His son, Fernando IV (1295–1312), was a sickly and ineffectual child king, not unlike the portrayal of the adolescent and indecisive Fernando I of the *Mocedades*. This is surely more than a coincidence and, in light of the ideological privileging of defiant Castilian nobles over monarchs in the poem, the portrayal of Fernando I as a weak and ineffectual child king suggests that the memory of the disastrous minority of Fernando IV influenced the narrative of Rodrigo's youthful adventures in the company of his king (Martin 1992, 464–7).

Rodrigo's heroic qualities are most apparent when in the company of his king, Fernando I. The contrast better emphasizes their differences, just as the mature Cid's heroism in the *Mio Cid* is highlighted by the depravity of his sons-in-law, the infantes de Carrión. Yet the late eleventh-century Latin *Carmen Campidoctoris* and the early twelfth-century Latin *Historia Roderici* confirm that the mature Cid was an exemplar of warrior virtue long before the infantes insinuated themsleves into the *Mio Cid*. Likewise, the young Rodrigo most likely was the subject of epic tales before his fate was joined to the immature King Fernando. In fact there is a brief mention of Rodrigo's youthful deeds in the *Historia Roderici* (chaps. 4–6), and the essential storyline of the *Mocedades* is recreated in the *Crónica de Castilla*, although in that version King Fernando is a mature and worthy king, much like his portrayal in other chronicles. At some point in the life of the narrative, Rodrigo's heroic qualities began to overwhelm the kingly virtues of Fernando I, presumably as the minorities of the sickly Fernando IV and his son Alfonso XI (one year old when his father died in 1312, he assumed the throne in 1325) impressed on the minds of their subjects the ineffectiveness of the monarchy in times of turmoil. The tale that emerged from those unfortunate experiences was crafted over many years by countless audiences who came to expect a story of Rodrigo that was more realistic in its depiction of the monarchs they had known. As a consequence, young Rodrigo's warrior ethos grew in direct proportion to the diminution of the royal family of Castile-León.

The model that may have suggested itself to minstrels as they reconfigured Rodrigo into a defiant, then a reluctant, vassal of King Fernando is the earliest of the legendary peninsular Christian warriors, Bernardo del Carpio. Bernardo's story is first recorded in the thirteenth-century Latin chronicle of Lucas, bishop of Tuy, the *Chronicon mundi* (ca. 1236), and soon after in a slightly different version in the history written by the bishop of Toledo, Rodrigo Jiménez de Rada, the *Historia de rebus Hispanie* (ca. 1242). Lucas tells us that Charlemagne had managed to drive the Muslims from France and then continued his march into northern Spain, taking a number of Christian cities. Emboldened by his success, Charlemagne wrote to Alfonso II, king of Asturias, making him his vassal. This enraged Bernardo alone among the nobles of the king's court, and in response Bernardo took part of the king's army and joined forces with Marsil, Muslim king of Zaragoza, against Charlemagne. Together they attacked the Frankish rearguard as they were returning to France through the mountain pass at Roncesvalles and annihilated them, killing Roland, prefect of Britanny, Count Anselm, Eggihard, overseer of Charlemagne's table, along with many other French nobles (Lucas, bk. 4, chap. 15).

The account of Bishop Rodrigo evidences a few new twists. Roland and his fellow nobles Anselm and Eggihard are leading the vanguard of Charlemagne's army into Spain. Bernardo and King Alfonso II, not the Muslim King Marsil, attack them straight on and annihilate them. Charlemagne, who was positioned farther back, sensed the destruction ahead of him and sounded the horn he was carrying, calling his men to retreat and regroup. They rushed back to Charlemagne, in part because they were expecting Bernardo and an army of Muslims to attack the rearguard, but Bernardo stayed in the front with Alfonso, annihilating the vanguard of the Frankish army (Jiménez de Rada, bk. 4, chap. 10).

The Alfonsine chroniclers translate and then struggle to combine the two Latin versions into a single narrative in the *Estoria de España*. Nothing of note is added, except for a reference to Charlemagne as 'Carlos, enperador de los romanos et de los alemanes et rey de los françeses' [Charles, emperor of the Romans and of the Germans and king of the French] (*Primera crónica general de España,* chap. 619). Similarly, in the *Mocedades*, letters demanding that Spain pay tribute to France are received by King Fernando from the king of France, the German emperor, and the Roman pope (ll. 805–6).

Additional parallels between the story of Bernardo del Carpio and the final episode of the *Mocedades* are noteworthy: the challenge to the sovereignty of a Spanish king delivered by letter, the lone angry response by the hero, and his successful armed retaliation against the French. Rodrigo's defiant attitude towards his king, fuelled in part by historical circumstances and modelled after an European myth of initiation, led minstrels to conflate Rodrigo's deeds with the earlier exploits of Bernardo del Carpio. Bernardo's will to freedom led minstrels to attribute to him the defeat of the French at Roncesvalles, providing Spanish audiences with an epic hero worthy of the warriors celebrated in the *Chanson de Roland.* Rodrigo, following in Bernardo's footsteps, led his king and countrymen to defeat the latter-day imperial ambitions of the French and, in the process, assimilated a narrative tradition of ancient myth and warrior ethos into a new historical reality.

A similar process accounts for the variant portrayals of King Fernando in the poem. When not in the company of Rodrigo, Fernando is a mature king who commands respect through his leadership and accomplishments on the battlefield. But when first Jimena and then Rodrigo enter the king's realm, he is an indecisive and fearful child prone to panic in the face of difficulties. The passages of the mature and accomplished king reflect an earlier narrative tradition of Fernando's exploits, some of which are historical, such as his struggle for power against his brothers, while others are fanciful, such as the peace he made with the sons of Laín Calvo. One passage composed of both fancy and history is the litany of his past deeds, including the invasion of France, narrated just as he and Rodrigo are about to cross the Pyrenees on their way to the gates of Paris (ll. 855–7). This hybrid figure, part history and part myth, indecisive child king and accomplished warrior, is aggravating to a modern reader of the poem, but it also provides good evidence of a vibrant narrative tradition, in constant flux and transformation. The same is true of Fernán

González and Rodrigo Díaz: the stories of their lives and deeds are not fixed, but through active engagement between minstrel and audience were constantly evolving in response to changing social circumstances.

Scholarship on the *Mocedades* does not readily acknowledge the dynamism of the oral tradition that produced this poem. There has been a tendency to try to pinpoint a specific moment in history or a concrete place and time that could have compelled an author to sit down and pen this work, suggesting a single voice and a social or political purpose as motivation for the work. But both the *Mocedades* and the *Mio Cid* are much too complex to surrender their secrets to such a limited concept of composition. They are the product of a rich and varied narrative tradition, responsible for their genesis and multiple later incarnations. They combine older, pre-existing narratives with emerging stories, familiar tales told in new contexts, well-rhymed passages committed to memory in the midst of others in which rhyme is fluctuating or has not yet been determined. The *Mocedades* is not nearly as well wrought as the *Mio Cid*, but its unfinished texture, the very crudeness of its composition, privileges us with insights into the aesthetics and mechanics of medieval epic composition in a way that the *Mio Cid*, for all its fine expression, could never do.

The *Mocedades* represents the last of the Spanish epic poems. The warrior world it celebrates is losing ground to a social reality that requires new skills and virtues, much more cerebral than physical or moral. Young Rodrigo is adapting, yet still retains some of the virtues of his forebears. His struggle to adapt is a universal one, of course, but he is young and full of promise. Rodrigo will soon abandon the epic mode altogether and become a shadow of his former self in Spain's celebrated Golden Age drama. But before this happens, there is one last chance to catch him at his best, in his *Mocedades*.

THE TEXT

The unique manuscript of the *Mocedades* is housed in the Bibliothèque Nationale de France, catalogued as Fonds Espagnol, 12. The copy is clearly legible with a few enlarged initials coloured with artistic flourish. The text is presented in two columns per folio, which is pleasing to the eye but fails to accommodate the line length required for the appropriate division of verses in a poetic text. In addition, the reading of the text is complicated by incongruence in the narration, uneven verse length, and inconsistent employment of assonance, all of which impede the determination of line division in the poem. Previous editors have assumed that the text was composed in writing, and that the author had the leisure and the inclination to produce lines with regular assonance. In this conception of the poem, the many cases of missing assonance are attributable to one or more copyists who, in transferring the text from one manuscript to another, paid little attention to the poetic qualities of the verse. In addition, one or another of these copyists had a particular interest in the genealogy of Rodrigo Díaz and in identifying the full names and titles of many of the protagonists in the poem. In an attempt to return the poem to its hypothetically pristine condition, some editors have engaged in a creative rewriting of the text by adding words to supply the missing assonance, especially noteworthy in the editions of Ramón Menéndez Pidal and Juan Victorio.

The present edition dispenses with the single-author conception of the poem and instead assumes that most passages in the text were composed orally and put into writing through dictation to a scribe. Oral dictation was the customary procedure for putting into writing the Latin and vernacular texts of the Middle Ages (Bailey 2003, 255–6; Menéndez Pidal 1924, 366–7). In addition, the text of the *Mocedades* bears the cognitive characteristics of oral discourse, such as the paratactic syntax of spontaneous speech, the absence of subordinating conjunctions, an absence of reflection or abstraction, and the frequent use of *e(t)* as a structuring device (Bakker 1997, 62–71).

The disposition of the text presented here is based on its presumed oral composition. Typically, this process involved scribes taking dictation from a minstrel onto wax tablets. An editorial process followed, in which one or more scribes, under the supervision of a cleric charged with the production of the text, selected passages from the dictated oral texts for transfer from the wax tablets onto parchment (Bailey 2003, 255–6; Duggan 2005). In the *Mocedades* it seems apparent that a variety of narratives were used. Some may have been recorded independently of the biography of Rodrigo's youth, and only later transferred to this new composition. This would be the case with the roughly one-quarter of the work that precedes the story of young Rodrigo as it traces the rise of the Castilian nation, including the extensive Fernán González story, and the Palencia material. The praise poem or *loor* to King Fernando is another passage that seems to be oral in its genesis and have been added to the larger *Mocedades* narrative as a written text (ll. 844–58). The manuscript text seems to reflect the processes of oral dictation, the editing and selection of diverse written texts, and the eventual final compositon of the more extensive narrative. A fairly complex process such as this would have been possible only under the guidance of a cleric, a learned man somewhat similar to the cleric from Palencia envisioned by Deyermond (1999, 14).

This conception of the poem informs all editorial decisions made here. For instance, the first folio of the text, some one hundred lines or so, is clearly not governed by assonance. In previous editions, this section was considered prose and organized into paragraphs. Closer examination reveals that it consists of a series of clause-like statements much like the half-lines of oral poetry, but instead of assonance marking the end of each line, *e(t)* 'and' marks the beginning. This compositional process is also evident in the earliest drafts of the vernacular prose chronicles of Castile. It is orally dictated text, and as such is represented here as single spurts of speech, structured by the repetition of *e(t)* at the beginning of each clause and assumed to be limited in length by the cognitive capabilities of short-term memory. Much like the verses that will soon begin to appear, each line is no more than a brief clause or two, composed of a small amount of information and joined to subsequent clauses in an adding-on or paratactic style. These are the characteristics of orally produced narrative, much like the examples of late twentieth-century spontaneous speech analysed by the linguist Wallace Chafe (1980, 20–9, for example). Medieval prose, in contrast, studiously avoids repetition and employs multiple subordinating conjunctions. It seems highly unlikely that the composer of these lines had in mind anything remotely related to a modern or medieval concept of prose. For these reasons, the first folio of the manuscript is presented with the same clause-like lines and numbers as the remainder of the text,

Some revisions made to the manuscript text are not indicated in the 'Notes to the Text,' such as eliminating unnecessary repetitions: *al rrey de de leon* (l. 12); standardizing the spelling of a name, such as *Fernand González* for *ferrnad gonçalez* (l. 31) and *ferrnand gonçalez* (l. 34); integrating a copyist's self-correction, as in *mantouo a (grand) castilla muy grant tiempo* (l. 32); filling in a missing letter, as when replacing *teniendo* with *tendiendo* (l. 47); or correcting an obvious copyist error, such as *abraçarlo* for *abraçarla* (l. 44), or copyist lapse as in *Camora* for *Çamora* (l. 412). Funes's edition provides a transcription of the manuscript text and identifies all corrections of this sort. To do the same here would be tediously repetitive for the editor and the reader. All revisions that clarify the meaning of the text, or that supply a missing word or phrase, are identified in the notes.

Modern punctuation is of course not found in medieval manuscripts. It has been added here to facilitate the reading of the text and includes capital letters, accent marks, commas, periods, a few exclamation points and question marks, as well as quotation marks used in representing speech. Since the text originated as oral discourse, the punctuation added here is meant to represent a continuous series of coordinated clauses. Punctuation is registered within the quotation marks in both the Spanish and English texts, for the sake of uniformity. Roman numerals are used sporadically in the manuscript text, and they have been written out in long form, as in *.dcccc.ᵒ* 'noveçientos' [nine hundred] (l. 1056), *.ccc.ᵒ* 'tresçientos' [three hundred] (l. 1078). *Et* 'and' [the Latinate form] is resolved as *e* [the vernacular form], including instances where it represents the letter *e*, such as *Etntre el rey Et el castellaño* (l. 1140). Ampersand (&), a symbol representing *e* 'and,' is also transcribed as *e*.

Editors of the *Mio Cid* and of the *Mocedades* organize lines by their shared assonance, so that a change in assonance requires a new *laisse* or *tirada*, separated and numbered as a distinct unit. This occurs numerous times in cases when there is no other indication of a pause or change in focus to justify a separation of lines. Some of the more sublime examples in Funes are the separation of lines 667–8, 671–2, 673–4, and 830–1 (here ll. 738–9, 742–3, 744–5, 903–4). Likewise, in instances where a change in focus is evident, but without a corresponding change in assonance, editors do not divide the verses into distinct passages. Textual divisions here represent major shifts in narrative focus, from the early Castilians to Rodrigo (ll. 345–6), and before each of Rodrigo's five battles (ll. 502–3, 572–3, 693–4, 789–90, 803–4).

Manuscript spellings have been preserved when they are recognizable in modern Spanish (*quando, commo, enbiar*), including variant spellings of many words, such as *vasallo/vassallo, pesar/pessar, lozano/loçano, llevar/levar,* etc. Instances of metathesis, *sacaldas, decilde,* etc., have not been altered. The letter *v* has been normalized in representing the consonantal sound, whereas the letter *u* stands for the vowel sound. The letter *i* has been reserved for the vowel sound, whereas the *j* is used as a palatal fricative consonant. The letter *y* as a consonant or semi-vowel is distinguished from the vowel sound represented by *i*, and is accented to represent the adverb *ý* (l. 86). On the few occasions when *y* is employed as a conjunction 'and,' it has been retained (ll. 862, 866–8). Double consonants such as *ff, rr, cc* have been simplified to reflect present-day use (*-rr-* has been reserved for intervocalic cases to represent the multiple vibrant, as in *tierra*). The *ç* is used in all instances of the voiceless alveolar affricate.

As is customary in current editorial practices, an apostrophe is used to indicate instances of vowel elision (*quel* > *que'l, fijo deste* > *fijo d'este*). Accent marks have been added in accordance with the norms of modern Spanish as pronunciation aids for Old Spanish. Word separation corresponds to modern Spanish usage. Examples include the separation of words joined in the manuscript (*dela* > *de la, enlos* > *en los, conel conde* > *con el conde*) and the joining of words separated in the manuscript, with the requisite accentuation added (*tomo lo la jnfanta* > *tomólo la infanta, medio dia* > *mediodía*). The many cases of vowel elision are indicated with an apostrophe, whether proclitic (*porque'l rey era rey de León*) or enclitic (*ol' daremos reino apartado, quel' dixieron*). Verbs with apocopated enclitic pronouns are accentuated as if the pronouns were whole (*plógol' al conde*).

Accentuation and word separation follow modern usage, even in cases in which the resultant word combinations are not found in modern Spanish

(*diógelo don Fernando, e comprógelo el rey*). Accentuation breaks from mod-
ern usage in some cases in which an unfamiliar word combination might cause
confusion (*tomólos de las manos, Recudióle Rodrigo*). Accentuation is also
used to distinguish a few instances of single-syllable homonyms that do not
exist in modern Spanish, such as the present indicative *é* in *irm'é para
Çamora* (l. 412), *á* in *arremeterl'ás* (l. 651), and *só* (modern Spanish *he, ha,
soy*), from the conjunction *e* (modern Spanish *y*), and from the prepositions *a,
so* (m. Sp. *a, bajo*); the present indicative *dó* (m. Sp. *doy*) and the interroga-
tives *dó, ó* (m. Sp. *dónde*) from the conjunctions *do, o*; the pronoun *ál* (m. Sp.
lo demás) to distinguish it from the contraction *al* (*a+el*); the stressed pro-
nouns *nós, vós* (m. Sp. *nosotros, vosotros*) versus the unstressed forms *nos,
vos* (m. Sp. *nos, os*). The word *mio* has not been accentuated, because its stress
seems to have varied. The imperfect indicative endings in *-ie* are accentuated
as diphthongs (*-ié, -iés, -ié, -iemos, -iedes, -ién*) as is the case when they are
used in the synthetic conditional (*avié, venién*).

THE TRANSLATION

Since the seminal study and paleographic edition of Alan Deyermond in 1969,
five critical editions of *Mocedades* have been published, the most recent being
that of Leonardo Funes (2004). The present edition draws a great deal from all
of them, but addresses a wider audience by presenting not only the Old Span-
ish text, but also an English translation of the text, with an introductory study,
notes to the text, and commentary also in English.

The translation is designed to recreate the experience of a medieval audience
hearing the poem for the first time. For that audience, comprehension would
have been immediate. Of course, to a speaker of modern Spanish the poem
seems archaic, the result of the unusual syntax and the archaic vocabulary and
verb forms employed in the poem. The English translation does not recreate the
archaic language of the poem, since for the medieval Castilian audience that lan-
guage was the one they spoke. In the same way, the modern English of the trans-
lation allows the reader to experience the immediate comprehension of the poem
and to sense directly the compelling dynamism of the story.

The translation does attempt to preserve the unusual syntax of the original
Spanish, something the medieval Castilian audience would have recognized as
unique to the oral discourse of the epic genre. This syntax results from the
constraints of oral verse making, especially the deployment of assonance in
the compositional process. Assonance is mostly a compositional aid employed
by minstrels in the production of oral narrative before an expectant audience.
For the minstrel and the audience, assonance marks the end of one line and the

beginning of another. Its use often requires the inversion of the syntax of standard speech, or repetition of fixed phrases to facilitate the ongoing assonance. The translation attempts to preserve the unique syntax and the characteristic repetition of this oral narrative as a means of privileging the reader with a direct acquaintance of the rhythm and the expression of the epic discourse of medieval Castile.

WORKS CITED

Alonso, D. 1954. *La primitiva épica francesa a la luz de una nota emilianense.* Madrid: CSIC, Instituto Miguel de Cervantes.

Alvar, C., and M. Alvar, eds. 1991. Mocedades de Rodrigo. In *Épica medieval española.* Madrid: Cátedra, 99–162.

Anon. Ca. 1083. *Carmen Campidoctoris o Poema latino del Campeador.* Eds. A. Montaner & Á. Escobar, 2001. Madrid: Sociedad Estatal España Nuevo Milenio.

– Ca. 1110. *Historia silense.* In Barton and Fletcher, eds., 2000, 9–64.

– 1284. *Crónica de veinte reyes.* Ed. C.H. Alonso, 1991. Burgos: Ayuntamiento.

– Ca. 1289. *Primera crónica general de España.* 2 vols. Ed. R. Menéndez Pidal, 1955. Madrid: Gredos.

– Ca. 1300. *Crónica de Castilla* (Passages relevant to the *Mocedades*). In Armistead, 1955, 116–58.

– 1344. *Crónica Geral de Espanha de 1344.* 4 vols. Ed. L.F. Lindley Cintra, 1951–90. Lisbon: Academia Portuguesa da História.

Armistead, S.G. 1955. *La gesta de las Mocedades de Rodrigo*: Reflections of a lost epic poem in the *Crónica de los reyes de Castilla* and the *Crónica General de 1344.* PhD diss., Princeton Univ. Abstract in *Dissertation Abstracts* 15, 2198–9.

– 1999. Las *Mocedades de Rodrigo* y el Romancero. In Bailey, ed., 1999, 19–36.

– 2000. *La tradición épica de las* Mocedades de Rodrigo. Salamanca: Ediciones Universidad.

Bailey, M. 1996. Las últimas hazañas del conde Fernán González en la *Estoria de España*: La contribución alfonsí. *La corónica* 24, no. 2: 31–40.

– ed. 1999. *Las* Mocedades de Rodrigo: *Estudios críticos, manuscrito y edición.* King's College London Medieval Studies, 15. London: King's College Centre for Late Antique and Medieval Studies.

– 1999. Vestigios del *Cantar de Fernán González* en las *Mocedades de Rodrigo.* In Bailey, ed., 1999, 89–97.

– 2003. Oral composition in the medieval Spanish epic. *PMLA* 118, no. 2: 254–69.

Bakker, E. 1997. *Poetry in speech.* Ithaca: Cornell University Press.

Barton, S., and R. Fletcher, eds. 2000. *The world of El Cid.* Manchester: Manchester University Press.

Catalán, Diego. 2000. Monarquía aristocrática y manipulación de las fuentes: Rodrigo en la *Crónica de Castilla*; El fin del modelo historiográfico alfonsí. In Martin, ed., 2000, 75–94.

Catholic encyclopedia. The cross and crucifix in liturgy: III; Festivals of the Holy Cross. http://www.newadvent.org/cathen/04533a.htm (accessed 22 Nov. 2006).

Chafe, W. 1980. The deployment of consciousness in the production of narrative. In *The pear stories: Cognitive, cultural, and linguistic aspects of narrative production.* Ed. W. Chafe, 9–50. Norwood: Ablex.

Deyermond, A. 1969. *Epic poetry and the clergy: Studies on the* Mocedades de Rodrigo. London: Tamesis.

– 1999. La autoría de las *Mocedades de Rodrigo*: Un replanteamiento. In Bailey, ed., 1999, 1–15.

Duggan, J. 2005. The interface between oral and written transmission of the *Cantar de Mio Cid. La corónica* 33, no. 2: 51–63.

Eco, U. 1986. *Travels in hyperreality.* Trans. W. Weaver. San Diego: Harcourt Brace Jovanovich.

Fernández-Ordóñez, I., ed. 1993. *Versión crítica de la* Estoria de España: *Estudio y edición desde Pelayo hasta Ordoño II.* Madrid: Seminario Menéndez Pidal, Universidad Complutense de Madrid.

– 2000. Variación en el modelo historiográfico alfonsí en el siglo XIII. In G. Martin, ed., 2000, 41–74.

Fletcher, R. 1989. *The quest for El Cid.* New York: Oxford Univ. Press.

Fradejas Lebrero, J. 1991. Estudio literario: Valores literarios de la *Crónica de veinte reyes.* In Anon., *Crónica de veinte reyes*, 31–51.

Funes, L., ed., with F. Tenenbaum. 2004. *Mocedades de Rodrigo:* Estudio y edición de los tres estados del texto. Woodbridge, UK: Tamesis.

Historia Roderici. Ca. 1110. In Barton and Fletcher, eds., 2000, 90–147.

Hook, D., and A. Long. 1999. Reflexiones sobre la estructura de las *Mocedades de Rodrigo.* In Bailey, ed., 1999, 53–67.

Huntington, A.M., ed. 1904. *Crónica rimada.* New York: n.p.

Jancovich, M. 2000. The purest knight of all: Nation, history, and representation in *El Cid* (1960). *Cinema Journal* 40, no. 1: 79–103.

Jiménez de Rada, R. Ca. 1242. *Historia de rebus hispanie sive Historia Gothica.* Ed. J. Fernández Valverde. 1987. Turnhout: Brepols.

López Guil, I., ed. 2001. *Libro de Fernán González.* Madrid: CSIC.

Lucas, bishop of Tuy. Ca. 1236. *Chronicon mundi.* Ed. E. Falque. 2003. Turnhout: Brepols.

Martin, G. 1992. *Les Juges de Castille: Mentalité et discours historique dans l'Espagne médiévale.* Annexes des *Cahiers de Linguistique Hispanique Médiévale*, 6. Paris: Séminaire d'Études Médiévales Hispaniques, Université de Paris-XIIII.

– ed. 2000. *La historia alfonsí: El modelo y sus destinos (siglos xiii–xv)*. Madrid: Casa de Velázquez.

Menéndez Pidal, R. 1924. *Poesía juglaresca y juglares: aspectos de la historia literaria y cultural de España*. Publicaciones de la *RFA*, 7. Madrid: Centro de Estudios Históricos.

– 1951. Cómo trabajaron las escuelas alfonsíes. *Nueva Revista de Filología Hispánica* 5:363–80.

Montgomery, T. 1984a. The lengthened lines of the *Mocedades de Rodrigo*. *Romance Philology*, 38, no. 1: 1–14.

– 1984b. Las *Mocedades de Rodrigo* y los romances. In *J.M. Solà-Solé: Homage, homenaje, homenatge* (Miscelánea de estudios de amigos y discípulos). Ed. A. Torres Alcalá. Barcelona: Puvill, 2:119–33.

– 1998. *Medieval Spanish epic: Mythic roots and ritual language*. University Park: Pennsylvania State Univ.

– 1999. Las *Mocedades* y el *Táin Bó Cúailnge*. In Bailey, ed., 1999, 37–51.

Ochoa, E. de. 1844. *Catálogo razonado de los manuscritos españoles existentes en la Biblioteca Real de París ...*, nº 9988 (as then numbered), 105–10. Paris: Imprenta Real.

Russell, P.E. 1958. San Pedro de Cardeña and the heroic history of the Cid. *Medium Aevum* 28, no. 2: 57–79.

Salvador Martínez, H., ed. 1991. *Poema de Fernán González*. Madrid: Espasa-Calpe.

Vaquero, Mercedes. 1999. Las *Mocedades* en el marco de la épica de revuelta española. In Bailey, ed., 1999, 99–136.

– 2005. The *Poema de Mio Cid* and the canon of the Spanish epic. *La corónica* 33, no. 2: 209–30.

Critical Editions (since Menéndez Pidal)

Alvar, C., and M. Alvar, eds. 1991. Mocedades de Rodrigo. In *Épica medieval española*. Madrid: Cátedra, 99–162.

Alvar, M., ed. 1969. *Cantar de Rodrigo y el rey Fernando*. In *Cantares de gesta medievales*, 123–80. México: Porrúa.

Funes, L., ed., with F. Tenenbaum. 2004. Mocedades de Rodrigo: *Estudio y edición de los tres estados del texto*. Woodbridge, UK: Tamesis.

Menéndez Pidal, R., ed. 1980. *Rodrigo y el rey Fernando*. In *Reliquias de la poesía épica española*. New introd. by Diego Catalán. Madrid: Cátedra-Seminario Menéndez Pidal & Gredos, 257–89. (Orig. pub. 1951.)

Victorio, J., ed. 1982. *Mocedades de Rodrigo*. Clásicos Castellanos, 226. Madrid: Espasa-Calpe.

Translations

Martin, G., ed. and trans. 2005. *Chansons de geste espagnoles: Chanson de Mon Cid, Chanson de Rodrigue.* Paris: Flammarion.

Semi-Paleographic Edition

Alfonso Pinto, F., ed. 1999. *Mocedades de Rodrigo. Las* Mocedades de Rodrigo. In Bailey, ed., 1999, 185–216.

Paleographic Transcription

Deyermond, A.D., ed. 1969. *Epic poetry and the clergy: Studies on the* Mocedades de Rodrigo. Colección Támesis. London: Tamesis, 221–77.

Bailey, Matthew, ed. 1994. *Texto y Concordancias de* Mocedades de Rodrigo (microfiche). Madison, WI: Hispanic Seminary of Medieval Studies.

Black and White Photographic Reproduction of Manuscript

Huntington, A.M., ed. 1904. *Crónica Rimada.* New York: n.p.

Colour Photographic Reproduction of Manuscript

In Bailey, ed., 1999, between 182 and 183.

LAS MOCEDADES DE RODRIGO

E remaneçió la tierra sin señor quando morió el rey Pelayo.   1
Este rey Pelayo avía una fija de ganançia,
e fue cassada con el conde don Suero de Casso,
e fizo en ella el conde don Suero un fijo que dixieron don Alfonso,
e a este don Alfón fizieron rey de León.   5
E los castellanos bevían en premia,
e avían guerra con Navarra e con Aragón,
e con los moros de Sant Estevan de Gormaz e de León e de
    Sepúlveda.
E era Olmedo de moros,
e dende adelante la tierra frontera que avía Castilla, Bilforado e
    Grañón,   10
e de la otra parte era Navarra frontera de León e de Carrión e de
    Saldaña.
E porque los castellanos ivan a cortes al rey de León con fijas e
    mugieres,
por esta razón fizieron en Castilla dos alcaldes,
e quando fuesse el uno a la corte, que'l otro manparasse la tierra.
¿Quáles fueron estos alcaldes?   15
El uno fue Nuño Rassura e el otro Laín Calvo.
¿E por qué dixieron Nuño Rasura este nonbre?
Porque cogió de Castilla señas eminas de pan,
e fizo voto a Santiago que les ayudasse contra los moros.
E el conde fue aqueste Nuño Rassura de Sant Pedro de Arlança.   20
E este Nuño Rasura ovo un fijo quel' dixieron Gonçalo Núñez,
e porque era malo e traviesso quíssolo el padre matar,
e fuesse para el rey moro Guiben, señor de Madrid.
E falló allá a doña Aldara Sánchez,
fija del rey don Sancho Ramírez de Navarra,   25
que andava mala mugier con los moros.
E pedióla por mugier, que acá non ge la darién,
e cassó con ella e tráxola a Castilla.
E fizo en ella tres fijos,
e los mayores non valieron nada,   30
e el menor fue el conde Fernand Gonçález.
que mantovo a Castilla muy grant tiempo.
E ovo de aver contienda con el rey don Sancho Ordóñez de Navarra.
E este rey don Sancho Ordóñez fizo vistas con el conde Fernand
    Gonçález,
en un lugar que dizen Vañárez.   35

E yendo el conde seguro, príssol' el rey en engaño,
e llevólo presso a Tudela de Navarra.
E yaziendo el conde presso, sacólo doña Costança,
hermana del rey don Sancho Ordóñez.
E yaziendo el conde en los fierros, tomólo la infanta a sus cuestas,   40
e dio con él en un monte.
E encontraron a un açipreste de aý, de Tudela de Navarra,
e dixo que si la infanta non le fiziesse amor de su cuerpo, que los
    descobrería.
E la infanta fue abraçarlo,
e teniéndole la infanta abraçado, llegó el conde con sus fierros,   45
e matólo con el su cochillo mismo del açipreste.
E tendiendo la infanta los ojos, vio venir grandes poderes,
e dixo al conde, 'Muertos somos, ¡mal pecado!,
ca haevos aquí los poderes del rey don Sancho mi hermano.'
E el conde tendió los ojos e fue los poderes devissando,   50
e conoçió los poderes e fue muy ledo e muy pagado,
e dixo a la infanta, 'Esta es Castilla, que me suele bessar la mano.'
E la infanta paró las cuestas,
e cavalgó muy privado en la mula del açipreste el conde,
e de pie iva la infanta,   55
e salió del monte privado.
E quando lo vieron los castellanos, todos se maravillaron,
mas nol' bessaron la mano nin señor nol' llamaron,
ca avían fecho omenaje a una piedra que traxieran en el carro,
que traían por señor fasta que fallaron al conde.   60
E tornaron la piedra a senblança del conde al Monte de Oca,
al logar donde la sacaron,
e todos al conde por señor le bessaron la mano.
E este conde Fernand Gonçález, después que en Castilla fue alçado,
mató al rey don Sancho Ordóñez de Navarra,   65
e él fuera en degollarlo con su mano.
E non quería obedeçer el conde a moro nin cristiano,
e enbiól' dezir al rey de León, fijo de don Suero de Casso,
don Alfonso avía por nonbre.
El rey enbió al conde enplazarlo,   70
quel' veniesse a vistas, e fue el conde muy pagado.
Cavalgó el conde commo omne tan lozano,
e a los treinta días contados fue el conde al plazo,
e el plazo fue en Saldaña.

E començóle él a preguntarlo, 75
'E yo maravillado me fago, conde, cómmo sodes ossado,
de non me venir a mis cortes nin me bessar la mano,
ca siempre fue Castilla de León tributario,
ca León es regno e Castilla es condado.'
Essas oras dixo el conde, 'Mucho andades en vano, 80
vós estades sobre buena mula gruessa e yo sobre buen cavallo.
Porque vos yo sofrí me fago mucho maravillado,
en aver señor Castilla e pedirle vós tributario.'
Essas oras dixo el rey, 'En las cortes será juzgado,
si obedeçerme devedes, si non, fincatvos en salvo.' 85
Essas oras dixo el conde, 'Lleguemos ý privado.'
En León son las cortes, llegó el conde lozano,
un cavallo lieva preçiado e un azor en la mano.
E conprógelo el rey por aver monedado,
en treinta e çinco mill maravedís fue el cavallo e el azor apreçiado. 90
Al gallarín ge lo vendió el conde, que ge lo pagasse a día de plazo.
Largos plazos passaron que non fue el conde pagado,
nin quirié ir a las cortes a menos de entregarlo.
Con fijos e con fijas e con mugieres, castellanos van a las cortes de
    León.
E conde Fernán González dixo al rey atanto, 95
'Rey, non verné a vuestras cortes a menos de ser pagado,
del aver que me devedes, de mi azor e de mi cavallo.'
Quando contaron el aver, el rey non podía pagarlo,
tanto creçió el gallarín que lo non pagaría el regnado.
Venieron abenençia el rey e el conde lozano, 100
que quitasse a Castilla, el conde fue mucho pagado,
plógol' al conde quando oyó este mandado.
Assí sacó a Castilla el buen conde don Fernando,
aviendo guerra con moros e con cristianos,
a toda parte de todo su condado. 105
Avía el conde un fijo que Garçi Fernández fue llamado.
Si el padre fue buen guerrero, el fijo fue atamaño.
Con fija de Almereque de Narbona, el conde Garçi Fernández fue
    cassado,
e con ella fizo un fijo que dixieron el conde don Sancho.
Quando a los siete años los infantes de Salas mataron, 110
morió el conde Garçi Fernández, cortés infançón castellano.
El buen conde don Sancho,

e dexóles buenos previllejos e buenos fueros con su mano.
E fue reçebir fija del rey de León, nieta del conde don Suero de
    Casso,
e en ella fizo un fijo quel' dixieron por nonbre Sancho.   115
Atanto salió de cazador al monte que'l non cogía el poblado.
Pússol' por nonbre el padre Sancho Avorta, por amor de destroir.
Desque vio el padre que era de edat, a Burgos fue llegado.
A los treinta días conplidos ayúntanse ý los castellanos.
Desque los vio el conde, en pie fue levantado,   120
'Oítme, castellanos, a buen tiempo só llegado,
por vos fazer más merçed que nunca vos fizo omne nado.
El conde Fernand Gonçález, mi avuelo, sacóvos de tributario,
el conde Garçi Fernández, mi padre,
e yo divos fueros e previllejos confirmados con mi mano.   125
De condado que es Castilla, fágovosla reinado.
Fagamos mio fijo Sancho Avarca rey, si vedes que es guissado.
Nieto es del rey de León, non ha quel' diga ome nado,
que non sea rey de Castilla, ninguno non será ossado,
si non, aquél quien lo dixiesse bien sabría vedarlo.'   130
Mucho plogo a castellanos quando oyeron este mandado.
A Sancho Avarca bessan las manos e '¡Real, real!' llamando,
por Castilla dan los pregones, por tan buen rey que alçaron.
Este fue el primero rey que castellanos ovieron,
con grand onra e grand prez grandes alegrías fezieron.   135
E el buen rey Sancho Avarca comenzó de reinar,
e mandó fazer señas tendidas en cada logar.
Con fija del rey de Françia se ovo a despossar,
e diógela de grado, non le fezieron ál.
E la infanta dizen doña Isabel, esta fue reina de prestar.   140
El rey don Sancho Avarca fue por ella, ca tiempo avía de cassar con
    ella.
A los puertos de Aspa ge la traxieron, e el rey de Françia,
e él allí fue a tomarla.
Grandes alegrías han en España quando el rey con la reina vieron
    tornar,
e mayor los castellanos quando la mano le fueron bessar.   145
E el conde don Pedro de Palençia, a Burgos le fue combidar,
'Rey don Sancho Avarca, por amor de caridat,
fijo del conde don Sancho, mi señor natural,
vayamos a Palençia, mio conbite tomar,

ca siempre vos serviré mientra mi vida durar.'   150
Dixo estonçe el rey bueno, 'Fazerlo he de grado,
en tal que en la mi vida nunca seades menguado.'
Esto fue nueve días ante de Sant Iohan,
quando el rey don Sancho llegó a Palençia yantar.
Bravo era el val de Palençia, ca non avía ý poblado,   155
sinon do llaman Santa María el Antigua, do morava el conde lozano.
Saliéronse a folgar, desque ovieron yantado,
e passaron las aguas amos de mano a mano.
Afondóse la mula con el rey en un soterraño,
acórrense las gentes e sacaron al rey en salvo,   160
por los braços quebró la mula, non la cavalgó más omne nado.
El rey tendió los ojos e vio por el soterraño,
desçender una escalera de un canto labrado.
Demandó por un cavallero que dezían Bernardo,
diz, 'Entra, Bernardo, por essa escalera e cata este soterraño.'   165
Dixo Bernaldo, 'Señor, plázeme de grado.'
Bernardo, quando desçendió, vio un pozo cavado,
e a par de aquel pozo vio estar un altar,
e de susso un escripto, e començólo de catar,
falló que Sant Antolín mártir yazía en aquel logar.   170
E vio una piedra con letras e començóla de catar,
e vio que treçientos años avía que era somido aquel logar.
E vínose para el rey e díxol' en poridat,
'Señor, commo me semeja, cuerpo santo yaze en este logar.'
Quando lo oyó el rey, al conde fue tornado,   175
e dixo, 'Ay, conde don Pedro, datme este logar en camio,
e siempre vos lo gradeçeré en quanto fuere durado,
e darvos he por él a Canpó fasta en la mar.'
Allí dixo el conde don Pedro al rey, 'Plázeme de grado.'
Danse las verdades e otorgáronse el cambio.   180
Estonçe traía el conde a çinco vandas las armas,
e las dos eran indias e las tres de oro colado.
Allí tomó otras el conde, el campo de oro claro,
una águila india en medio gritando.
'¡Campó!' ivan llamando.   185
Por esso llaman Aguilar de Canpó, desque él erzió condado.
El rey en plazentería fincó alegre e pagado.
Llegáronle mandados de su avuelo el rey de León, que era finado.
Fincáronle tres fijas e non fijo varón.

Ca el rey con la una fue cassado,   190
e el conde don Ossorio galeçiano con la otra,
el que fizo don Ordoño de Campos mucho onrado.
E la otra con el conde Nuño Álvarez de Amaya, que ovo a Amaya
   por condado.
E fincaron en el rey don Sancho Avarca todos los reinos en su mano.
E dixo a su cavallero Bernardo que catasse el soterraño.   195
E oiredes lo que aconteçió estonçe en aquel año.
Estando el arçobispo en el pueblo toledano,
en día de Ramos, en Visagra la missa cantando,
a la ora de la Passión entraron moros el poblado,
e ganaron a Toledo, a menos del poblado,   200
e guareçió el arçobispo a poder de cavallo.
Aportó en Palençia, a donde está Bernardo,
siendo Bernardo su sobrino, fijo de su hermano.
Quando vio al arçobispo, dexó el soterraño,
e fuesse para Defessa Brava, meterse hermitaño,   205
en una hermita, que avía ý otro poblado.
Miro, quando vio este lugar, cavalgó muy privado.
Fuesse para León, al buen rey don Sancho,
de los ojos llorando e bessóle la mano,
'Señor rey don Sancho Avarca, por el Padre apoderado,   210
perdí a Toledo, moros me lo han ganado.
Señor, datme a Palençia e a aquel soterraño,
e faré vida de que Dios sea pagado,
de arçobispo que era, biviré commo hermitaño.'
E en essas horas dixo el rey, 'Plázeme muy de grado.'   215
Apriessa dixo, 'Mio señor, itme a entregarlo.'
E entrante a Palençia tomólo por la mano,
'Commo lo yo conpré del conde don Pedro, franco dólo de grado.
E fagan un previllegio con mio signo otorgado,
de la Huerta del Campo, do es Oter Redondo llamado,   220
con las cuestas del Atalaya e de los Cascajares del Bravo,
e de la otra parte, las cuestas commo van a Valroçiado.'
Muy bien lo reçibe Miro el perlado.
E tomó el previlejo del rey e cavalgó muy privado,
e metiósse a los caminos, para Roma fue llegado.   225
E quando vio al papa, el pie le ovo bessado,
'Merçed,' dixo, 'señor, que sodes en lugar de Sant Pedro e Sant
   Pablo.

Siendo yo arçobispo del pueblo toledano,
conqueriéronme los moros, onde fue muy coitado.
Víneme para el rey don Sancho Avarca, fijo del conde don Sancho,   230
commo a omne de buena ventura que en buen punto fue nado.
En el val de Palençia abrióse un soterraño,
e afondóse la mula e él fincó en sano.
A Sant Antolín mártir fallaron ý soterrado,
apriessa lo conpró luego el rey de un conde lozano.   235
Quando yo perdí a Toledo, a mí lo ovo dado el rey,
ahevos aquí su previllejo, commo lo trayo otorgado.'
El papa, quando vio el previllejo con signo acabado,
dixo, 'Fizo commo rey de buena ventura en fazer tan buen logar
    franqueado.
Fagamos ý una dignidat de que Dios sea pagado.   240
Pues lo dieron a la Iglesia, de mí sea otorgado,
a ti, Miro, episcopus palentino mucho onrado.'
Quando estos previllejos el obispo del papa ovo tomado,
a jornadas contadas a España fue tornado.
Sópolo el rey don Sancho Avarca e reçebiólo muy de grado.   245
Entrante Oter Redondo tomólo el rey por la mano,
fasta Sant Antolín non quisso dexallo.
E dixo, 'Yo vos la franqueo ansí commo vos lo yo ove dado.
Fijo que yo aya que fuere en demandarlo,
la mi maldezión aya e non le ayude omne nado,   250
e el que lo ayudare sea traidor provado,
e de parte de la Iglesia maldito sea e descomulgado,
e dó el poder a la Iglesia con mi sello colgado.'
Porque'l rey era rey de León, desmanparó a castellanos,
e vedes por quál razón, porque era León cabeza de los reinados.   255
Alçósele Castilla e duró bien diez e siete años.
Alçáronssele los otros linajes d'onde venían los fijos dalgo.
¿D'ónde son estos linajes? Del otro alcalde Laín Calvo.
¿D'ónde fue este Laín Calvo? Natural de Monte de Oca.
E vino a Sant Pedro de Cardeña a poblar, este Laín Calvo,   260
con quatro fijos que llegaron a buen stado.
Con seisçientos cavalleros a Castilla manpararon.
Aviendo guerra con Navarra, Ruy Laínez, el mayor, pobló a Faro.
Galduy Laínez, d'ése ovo a Mendoça e Treviño poblado,
aviendo guerra con moros, donde reçebieron grand daño.   265
Siendo Sant Estevan de Gormaz de moros, e León del otro cabo,

e Atienza e Çigüença, con que bivién castellanos en trabajo,
Sepúlveda e Olmedo, de un moro pagano,
a pessar de aquestos todos, un fijo de Laín Calvo,
a quel' dizen Peñaflor, con qual es Peñafiel llamado.   270
Aviendo guerra con el rey de León e con leonesses,
el menor de Laín Calvo, quel' dixieron Diego Laínez,
éste ovo a Saldaña por frontera grand tiempo passado.
Ovo a morir el rey Sancho Avarca, estando la tierra en este
    trabajo.
Tres fijos dexó el rey el día que fue finado.   275
Con Alfonso, el mayor, leonesses se alzaron,
e don Garçía, el mediano, a Navarra fue alçado.
Por señor le tomaron a don Fernando, el menor,
la mano le bessaron castellanos, commo fijos de Laín Calvo.
Dio guerra a sus hermanos.   280
Vençidos fueron leonesses e reçebieron grand daño.
A los fitos de Mansilla, do estavan los mojones fincados,
mató don Fernando a don Alfonso su hermano.
Luego se le dieron leoneses e Galizia fasta Santiago.
Tornó dar guerra a Navarra, commo de cabo,   285
e mató en Atapuerca a don Garçía su hermano.
Diósele luego Navarra e Aragón del otro cabo.
Desde allí se llamó señor de España fasta en Santiago.
Preguntó por Navarra, si avía quién heredarlo.
Fabló la infanta doña Sancha, fija del rey don Sancho,   290
e el governador de Navarra,
e fabló el infante don Ramiro, mas non era de velada.
Mas por quanto era fijo d'este rey don Sancho,
e que non se enagenasse el reino, diógelo don Fernando.
Assí assosegó su tierra, a Çamora fue llegado,   295
mandando por sus reinos que veniessen a sus cortes a los treinta días
    contados.
Allí vinién leonesses e con gallizianos e con asturianos,
e venieron aragonesses a bueltas con navarros.
Los postrimeros fueron castellanos e estremadaños.
De los fijos de Laín Calvo, todos quatro hermanos.   300
Don Ruy Laínez fue cassado con fija de don Gonzalo Minayas,
e fizo en ella a don Diego Ordoñes,
donde vienen éstos que de Vizcaya son llamados.
Galdín Laínez fue cassado con fija del conde don Rodrigo,

el conde de Alva e de Vitoria,   305
e fizo en ella un fijo quel' dezían don Lope,
donde vienen estos Laínez, de don Luis Díaz de Mendoça.
El infante Laínez era cassado con fija del conde don Álvaro de
    Feuza,
e fizo en ella un fijo que dixieron Álvar Fáñez,
donde vienen estos linajes de Castro.   310
Diego Laínez se ovo cassado con doña Theresa Núñez,
fija del conde Ramón Álvarez de Amaya e nieta del rey de León,
e fizo en ella un fijo quel' dixieron el buen guerreador Ruy Díaz.
Allí se levantó el rey.
A los quatro fijos de Laín Calvo tomólos por las manos,   315
consigo los puso en el estrado,
'Oítme, cavalleros, muy buenos fijos dalgo,
del más onrado alcalde que en Castilla fue nado.
Dístesme a Castilla e bessástesme la mano,
convusco conquerí los reinos de España fasta Santiago.   320
Vós sodes ançianos e yo del mundo non sé tanto.
Mi cuerpo e mi poder métolo en vuestras manos,
que vós me consejedes sin arte e sin engaño.
Rey soy de Castilla e de León, assí fago.
Sabedes que León es cabeza de todos los reinados,   325
e por esso vos ruego e a vós pregunto tanto,
quál seña me mandades fazer, atal faré de grado,
ca en quanto yo valga non vos saldré de mandado.'
Dixieron los castellanos, 'En buen punto fuestes nado.
Mandat fazer un castillo de oro e un león indio gritado.'   330
Mucho plogo al rey quando los reinos se pagaron.
Bien ordenó el rey su tierra, commo rey mucho acabado.
Otorgó todos los fueros que el rey su padre avía dado.
Otorgó los previllejos de su avuelo, el conde don Sancho.
Allí llegó de Palençia el mandado que era muerto el obispo Miro.   335
E dio el obispado a Bernardo,
e enbiól' quel' confirmase a Roma,
e vino muy buen perlado.
E otorgó sus libertades que el rey Sancho Avarca avía dado,
desde la Huerta del Topo fasta do es la Quintanilla con todo,   340
fasta Castiel Redondo, do es Magaz llamado,
detrás de las Cuestas de los Cascajares, do es Santo Thomé llamado,
fasta las otras cuestas que llaman Val Royado,

do llaman Val de Pero, ca non era poblado.
Mandó en los previllejos poner signo el buen rey don Fernando.   345

Asosegada estava la tierra, que non avié guerra de ningún cabo.
El conde don Gómez de Gormaz a Diego Laínez fizo daño,
frióle los pastores e robóle el ganado.
A Bivar llegó Diego Laínez, al apellido fue llegado.
Él enbiólos reçebir a sus hermanos e cavalga muy privado.   350
Fueron correr a Gormaz, quando el sol era rayado.
Quemáronle el arraval e comenzáronle el andamio,
e trae los vassallos e quanto tienen en las manos,
e trae los ganados, quantos andant por el campo,
e tráele por dessonra las lavanderas, que al agua están lavando.   355
Tras ellos salió el conde con çient cavalleros fijos dalgo,
rebtando a grandes bozes a fijo de Laín Calvo,
'¡Dexat mis lavanderas, fijo del alcalde çibdadano,
c'a mí non me atenderedes atantos por tantos!,'
por quanto él está escalentado.   360
Redró Ruy Laínez, señor que era de Faro,
'Çiento por çiento vos seremos de buena miente e al pulgar.'
Otórganse los omenajes, que fuessen ý al día de plazo.
Tórnanle de las lavanderas e de los vassallos,
mas non le dieron el ganado,   365
ca se lo querién tener, por lo que el conde avía levado.
A los nueve días contados cavalgam muy privado.
Rodrigo, fijo de don Diego e nieto de Laín Calvo,
e nieto del conde Nuño Álvarez de Amaya,
e visnieto del rey de León.   370
Doze años avía por cuenta e aún los treze non son,
nunca se viera en lit, ya quebrávale el coraçón.
Cuéntasse en los çien lidiadores, que quisso el padre o que non,
en los primeros golpes suyos e del conde don Gómez son.
Paradas están las hazes e comienzan a lidiar,   375
Rodrigo mató al conde, ca non lo pudo tardar.
Venidos son los çiento e pienssan de lidiar,
en pos ellos salió Rodrigo, que los non da vagar.
Prisso a dos fijos del conde, a todo su mal pessar,
a Fernán Gómez e Alfonso Gómez, e tráxolos a Bivar.   380
Tres fijas avía el conde, cada una por casar.
E la una era Elvira Gómez,

e la mediana Aldonza Gómez,
e a la otra Ximena Gómez, la menor.
Quando sopieron que eran pressos los hermanos e que era muerto el
    padre,												385
paños visten brunitados e velos a toda parte.
Estonçe la avían por duelo, agora por gozo la traen.
Salen de Gormaz e vanse para Bivar.
Violas venir don Diego e a reçebirlas sale,
'¿D'ónde son aquestas freiras, que algo me vienen demandar?'					390
'Dezirvos hemos, señor, que non avemos por qué vos lo negar.
Fijas somos del conde don Gormaz, e vós le mandastes matar,
prissístesnos los hermanos e tenédeslos acá,
e nós mugieres somos, que non ay quién nos anpare.'
Essas oras dixo don Diego, 'Non devedes a mí culpar,							395
peditlas a Rodrigo, si vos las quesiere dar,
prométolo yo a Cristus, a mí non me puede pessar.'
Aquesto oyó Rodrigo, comenzó de fablar,
'Mal fezistes, señor, de vós negar la verdat,
que yo seré vuestro fijo e seré de mi madre.							400
Parat mientes al mundo, señor, por caridat,
non han culpa las fijas por lo que fizo el padre.
Datles a sus hermanos, que muy menester los han,
contra estas dueñas mesura devedes catar.'
Allí dixo don Diego, 'Fijo, mandátgelos dar.'							405
Sueltan los hermanos, a las dueñas los dan.
Quando ellos se vieron fuera en salvo comenzaron de fablar.
Quinze días possieron de plazo a Rodrigo e a su padre,
'Que los vengamos quemar de noche en las cassas de Bivar.'
Fabló Ximena Gómez, la menor,									410
'Mesura,' dixo, 'hermanos, por amor de caridat.
Irm'é para Çamora, al rey don Fernando querellar,
e más fincaredes en salvo e él derecho vos dará.'
Allí cavalgó Ximena Gómez, tres donçellas con ella van,
e otros escuderos que la avían de guardar.							415
Llegava a Zamora, do la corte del rey está,
llorando de los ojos e pediéndol' piedat,
'Rey, dueña só lazrada e áveme piedat,
orphanilla finqué pequeña de la condessa mi madre.
Fijo de Diego Laínez fízome mucho mal,							420
príssome mis hermanos e matóme a mi padre.

A vós que sodes rey véngome a querellar.
Señor, por merçed, derecho me mandat dar.'
Mucho pessó al rey e començó de fablar,
'En grant coita son mis reinos, Castilla alçárseme ha,   425
e si se me alçan castellanos, fazerme han mucho mal.'
Quando lo oyó Ximena Gómez, las manos le fue bessar,
'Merçed,' dixo, 'señor, non lo tengades a mal,
mostrarvos he assosegar a Castilla e a los reinos otro tal.
Datme a Rodrigo por marido, aquel que mató a mi padre.'   430
Quando aquesto oyó el conde don Ossorio, amo del rey don
    Fernando,
tomó el rey por las manos e aparte iva sacallo,
'Señor, ¿qué vos semeja?, ¡qué don vos ha demandado!
Mucho lo devedes agradeçer al Padre apoderado.
Señor, enbiat por Rodrigo e por su padre privado.'   435
Apriessa fazen las cartas, que non lo quieren tardar.
Danlas al mensajero, al camino es entrado.
Quando llegó a Bivar, don Diego estava folgando.
Dixo, 'Omíllome a vós, señor, ca vos trayo buen
    mandado,
enbía por vós e por vuestro fijo el buen rey don Fernando.   440
Vedes aquí sus cartas firmadas que vos trayo,
que si Dios quesiere, será aína Rodrigo ençimado.'
Don Diego cató las cartas e ovo la color mudado,
sospechó que por la muerte del conde quería el rey matarlo.
'Oítme,' dixo, 'mi fijo, mientes catedes acae,   445
témome de aquestas cartas que andan con falsedat,
e d'esto los reys muy malas costumbres han.
Al rey que vós servides, servillo muy sin arte,
assí vós aguardat d'él commo de enemigo mortal.
Fijo, passat vós para Faro, do vuestro tío Ruy Laínez está,   450
e yo iré a la corte do el buen rey está,
e si a por aventura el rey me matare,
vós e vuestros tíos poderme hedes vengar.'
Allí dixo Rodrigo, 'E esso non sería la verdat,
por lo que vós passaredes, por esso quiero yo passar.   455
Maguer sodes mi padre, quiérovos yo aconsejar.
Treçientos cavalleros todos convusco los levat,
a la entrada de Çamora, señor, a mí los dat.'
Essa ora dixo don Diego, 'Pues pensemos de andar.'

Métense a los caminos, para Çamora van.   460
A la entrada de Çamora, allá do Duero cay,
ármanse los trezientos e Rodrigo otro tale.
Desque los vio Rodrigo armados, començó de fablar,
'Oítme,' dixo, 'amigos, parientes e vasallos de mi padre.
Aguardat vuestro señor sin engaño e sin arte.   465
Si viéredes que el alguazil lo quisiere prender, mucho apriessa lo
   matat.
Tan negro día aya el rey commo los otros que aý están.
Non vos pueden dezir traidores por vós al rey matar,
que non somos sus vasallos, nin Dios non lo mande.
Que más trayador sería el rey si a mi padre matasse   470
por yo matar mi enemigo en buena lid en campo.'
Irado va contra la corte do está el buen rey don Fernando,
todos dizen, 'Ahé'l que mató al conde loçano.'
Quando Rodrigo bolvió los ojos, todos ivan derramando.
Avién muy grant pavor d'él, e muy grande espanto.   475
Allegó don Diego Laínez al rey bessarle la mano.
Quando esto vio Rodrigo non le quisso bessar la mano.
Rodrigo fincó los inojos por le bessar la mano,
el espada traía luenga, el rey fue mal espantado,
a grandes bozes dixo, '¡Tiratme allá esse pecado!'   480
Dixo estonçe don Rodrigo, 'Querría más un clavo,
que vós seades mi señor, nin yo vuestro vassallo.
Porque vos la bessó mi padre, soy yo mal amanzellado.'
Essas oras dixo el rey al conde don Ossorio, su amo,
'Dadme vós acá essa donçella, despossaremos este lozano.'   485
Aún non lo creyó don Diego, tanto estava espantado.
Salió la donçella e tráela el conde por la mano.
Ella tendió los ojos e a Rodrigo comenzó de catarlo,
dixo, 'Señor, muchas merçedes, ca éste es el conde que yo
   demando.'
Allí despossavan a doña Ximena Gómez con Rodrigo el Castellano.   490
Rodrigo respondió muy sañudo contra el rey castellano,
'Señor, vós me despossastes más a mi pessar que de grado,
mas prométolo a Cristus que vos non besse la mano,
nin me vea con ella en yermo nin en poblado,
fasta que venza çinco lides en buena lid en canpo.'   495
Quando esto oyó el rey fízose maravillado,
dixo, 'Non es éste omne, mas figura ha de pecado.'

Dixo el conde don Ossorio, 'Mostrarvos lo he privado.
Quando los moros corrieren a Castilla, non le acorra omne nado,
veremos si lo dize de veras o si lo dize bafando.'   500
Allí espedieron padre e fijo, al camino fueron entrados.
Fuesse para Bivar, a Sant Pedro de Cardeña, por morar ý el verano.

Corrió el moro Burgos de Ayllón muy lozano,
e el arrayaz Bulcor de Sepúlveda muy honrado,
e su hermano Tosios, el arrayaz de Olmedo, muy rico e mucho
     abondado.   505
Entre todos eran çinco mill moros a cavallo.
E fueron correr a Castilla e llegaron a Bilforado,
e quemaron a Redezilla e a Grañón de cabo a cabo.
A Rodrigo llegó el apellido quando en siesta estava adormido.
Defendió que ninguno non despertasse a su padre, sol non fuesse
     ussado.   510
Métense a las armas e cavalgan muy privado.
Trezientos cavalleros del padre vanlo aguardando,
e otras gentes de Castilla que se le ivan llegando.
E los moros venién robando la tierra e faziendo mucho daño,
traían grant poder, con robo de ganado,   515
e cristianos captivos, ¡mal pecado!
A la Nava del Grillo, do es Lerma llamado,
allí los alcançó Rodrigo, seguiólos en alcançe.
Lidió con los algareros, que non con los que levavan el ganado,
e a los unos mató e a los otros fue arramando.   520
Por el campo de Gomiel a Yoda llegaron,
do ivan los poderes con el robo tamaño.
Allí lidió Rodrigo con ellos buena lid en el campo,
un día e una noche, fasta otro día mediado,
e estudo en pesso la batalla e el torneo mesclado.   525
Rodrigo vençió la batalla, ¡Dios sea loado!
Fasta Peña Falcón, do es Peñafiel llamado,
las aguas de Duero ívanlas enturbiando.
Allí bolvieron un torneo, contra Fuentedueña llegando.
Mató Rodrigo a los dos arrayazes e prisso al moro Burgos
     loçano.   530
E traxo los paganos contra Tudela de Duero, e el ganado,
captivos e captivas tráxolos el castellano.
En Çamora llegaron los mandados,

do era el buen rey don Fernando.
El rey quando lo sopo fue ledo e pagado.   535
¡Ay Dios, qué grande alegría fazía el rey castellano!
Cavalgó el buen rey, con él muchos condes e cavalleros e otros
    omnes fijos dalgo.
Fuese para Tudela de Duero, do paçía el ganado.
Rodrigo quandol' vio venir, reçebiólo muy privado,
'Cata,' dixo, 'buen rey, qué te trayo, maguera non só tu vassallo.   540
De çinco lides que te prometí el día que tú me oviste desposado,
vençido he la una, yo cataré por las quatro.'
Essas oras dixo el buen rey, 'Por todo seas perdonado,
en tal que me dés el quinto de quanto aquí has ganado.'
Estonçe dixo Rodrigo, 'Solamente non sea pensado,   545
que yo lo daré a los mesquinos, que assaz lo han lazrado.
Lo suyo daré a los diezmos, que non quiero su pecado.
De lo mio daré soldadas a aquellos que me aguardaron.'
Essas oras dixo el buen rey, 'Dame a esse moro lozano.'
Estonçe dixo Rodrigo, 'Solamente non sea pensado,   550
que non, por quanto yo valgo,
que fidalgo a fidalgo, quandol' prende, non deve dessonrarlo.
De más non vos daré el quinto, sinon de aver monedado,
que darlo he a mis vassallos, que assaz me lo han lazerado.'
Despediéronse del rey e bessáronle la mano.   555
Trezientos cavalleros fueron por cuenta, los que allí fueron
    juntados.
Quando esto vio Rodrigo, a los moros se tornó privado,
'Oítmelo, rey moro Burgos de Ayllón muy lozano.
Yo non prendería rey, nin a mí non sería dado,
mas roguévos que veniésedes conmigo, vós fezísteslo de grado.   560
Itvos para vuestro reinado salvo e seguro,
que en toda la mi vida non ayades miedo de rey moro nin de
    cristiano.
Quanto avían los arrayazes que yo maté, vós heredatlo,
si vos quesieren abrir las villas, si non, enbiatme mandado,
yo faré que vos abran a miedo, que non de grado.'   565
Quando esto vio el moro Burgos de Ayllón muy lozano,
fincó los inojos delante Rodrigo e bessóle la mano,
de boca fablando, 'A ti digo el mi señor, yo só el tu vassallo,
e dóte de mi aver el quinto e tus parias en cada año.'
Alegre se va el moro, alegre se tornó el castellano.   570

Parias le enbió el rey moro de Ayllón muy lozano,
que para en quatro años fuesse rico e abondado.

Sópolo el conde don Martín Gonçález de Navarra, cavalgó muy
　　privado,
e fuesse para el rey, 'Señor, péssete del tu daño.
Calahora e Tudela forçada te la ha el buen rey don Fernando.　　575
Señor, dame tus cartas e iré desafiarlo,
yo seré tu justador, conbaterlo he privado.'
Essas horas dixo el rey, 'Séate otorgado.'
Las cartas dan al conde, al camino es entrado,
allegava a Çamora, al buen rey don Fernando.　　580
Entró por la corte, al buen rey bessó la mano,
e dixo, 'Oítme, rey de grand poder, un poco sea escuchado,
mensagero con cartas non deve tomar mal nin reçebir daño.
Enbíavos desafiar el rey de Aragón, a vós e a todo vuestro reinado,
vedes aquí sus cartas, yo vos trayo el mandado.　　585
Si non, datme un justador de todo vuestro reinado,
yo lidiaré por el rey de Aragón, que só su vassallo.'
Quando esto oyó el rey, en pie fue levantado,
e dixo, 'Pessar devía a Dios e a todo su reinado,
de tal cossa começar rey que devía ser su vassallo.　　590
¿Quién ge lo consejó? e ¿cómmo fue de ello ossado?
¿Quál sería de mis reinos, amigo o pariente o vassallo,
que por mí quessiese lidiar este rieto?'
Rodrigo, a los tres días a Çamora ha llegado.
Vio estar al rey muy triste, ante él fue parado,　　595
sonrisándose iva e de la boca fablando,
'Rey que manda a Castilla e a León non deve ser desconortado.
Rey, ¿quién vos fizo pessar? o ¿cómmo fue d'ello ossado?
De presso o de muerto non vos saldrá de la mano.'
Essas horas dixo el rey, 'Seas bienaventurado,　　600
a Dios mucho agradesco por ver que eres aquí llegado.
A ti digo la mi coita, donde soy coitado.
Enbióme desafiar el rey de Aragón e nunca ge lo ove buscado,
enbióme dezir quel' diesse a Calahorra, amidos o de grado,
o quel' diesse un justador de todo el mi regnado.　　605
Querelléme en mi corte a todos los fijos dalgo,
non me respondió omne nado,
Respóndele tú, Rodrigo, mi pariente e mi vassallo,

fijo eres de Diego Laínez e nieto de Laín Calvo.'
Essas horas dixo Rodrigo, 'Señor, pláçeme de grado. 610
Atal plazo nos dedes que pueda ser tornado,
que quiero ir en romería al padrón de Santiago,
e a Santa María de Rocamador, si Dios quesiere guissarlo.'
Essas horas dixo el rey, 'En treinta días avrás afarto.'
El conde con grand bigor, en pie fue levantado, 615
e dixo, 'Rey, en treinta días mucho es grand plazo,
que más me quería ver con Rodrigo que quien me diesse un
    condado.'
Estonçe dixo Rodrigo, 'Conde, ¿por qué vós quexades tanto?
Que a quien diablos han de tomar, chica es posiesta de mayo.'
Essas horas dixo el rey, 'Ve tu vía, bienaventurado.' 620
A los caminos entró Rodrigo, passól' a Malgrado,
de qual dizen Benabente, segunt dize en el romançe,
e passó por Astorga e llegó a Monte Iraglo.
Complió su romería, por Sant Salvador de Oviedo fue tornado,
a la condessa doña Theresa Núñez, e apriessa ovo preguntado, 625
'Señora, ¿quántos días ha passados que yo fue en romería a
    Santiago?'
E dixo la condessa, 'Oy passan veinte e seis días,
cras serán los veinte e siete días llegados.'
Quando esto oyó Rodrigo fue mal amanzellado,
e dixo, 'Cavalgat, mis cavalleros, e non querades tardarlo, 630
vayámosnos servir al buen rey don Fernando,
que tres días ha, non más, para complirse el plazo.'
A los caminos entró Rodrigo con treçientos fijos dalgo.
Al vado de Cascajar, a do Duero fue apartado,
fuerte día fazía de frío, a la posiesta en llegando. 635
A la horilla del vado estava un pecador de malato,
a todos pediendo piedat, que le passasen el vado.
Los cavalleros todos escopían e ívanse d'él arredrando.
Rodrigo ovo d'él duelo e tomólo por la mano,
so una capa verde aguadera passólo por el vado, 640
en un mulo andador que su padre le avía dado.
E fuesse para Grejalva, do es Çerrato llamado,
so unas piedras cavadas, que era el poblado.
So la capa verde aguadera, alvergó el castellano e el malato,
e en siendo dormiendo, a la oreja le fabló el gapho, 645
'¿Dormides, Rodrigo de Bivar? Tiempo has de ser acordado,

mensagero só de Cristus, que non soy malato.
Sant Lázaro só, a ti me ovo Dios enbiado,
que te dé un resollo en las espaldas, que en calentura seas entrado,
que quando esta calentura ovieres, que te sea menbrado,   650
quantas cossas comenzares, arrematarl'ás con tu mano.'
Diol' un resollo en las espaldas, que a los pechos le ha passado,
Rodrigo despertó e fue muy mal espantado,
cató en derredor de sí e non pudo fallar el gapho,
menbróle d'aquel sueño e cavalgó muy privado.   655
Fuesse para Calahorra, de día e de noche andando.
Ý era el rey don Ramiro de Aragón,
ý era el rey don Fernando,
ý era el rey don Ordoño de Navarra.
Venido era el día del plaço e non assomava el castellano.   660
En priessa se vio el rey, e a Diego Laínez ovo buscado,
'Diego Laínez, vós lidiat este rieto por salvar a vuestro fijo, que a
     vós era dado.'
Dixo Diego Laínez, 'Señor, plázeme de grado.'
Ármanle mucho apriessa el cuerpo e el cavallo,
quando quisso cavalgar, assomó el castellano.   665
A reçebirle sale el rey con muchos fijos dalgo,
'Adelante,' dixo a Rodrigo, '¿por qué tardades tanto?'
Estonçe dixo Rodrigo, 'Señor, non sea culpado,
ca aún fasta el sol puesto es todo el día mi plazo.
Lidiaré en esse cavallo de mi padre, que el mio viene muy cansado.'   670
Dixo Diego Laínez, 'Fijo, plázeme de grado.'
El rey con grant plazer parósse armarlo.'
Dixo Rodrigo, 'Señor, non sea culpado.'
Cavalgar quería Rodrigo, non quería tardarlo.
Non le venía la calentura que le avía dicho el malato,   675
dixo al rey, 'Señor, dadme una sopa en vino.'
Quando quisso tomar la sopa, la calentura ovo llegado,
en logar de tomar la sopa, tomó la rienda del cavallo.
Enderezó el pendón e el escudo ovo enbrazado,
e fuesse para allí do estava el Navarro.   680
El navarro llamó '¡Aragón!' e '¡Castilla!' el castellano,
ívanse dar seños golpes, los cavallos encostaron.
Dixo el conde navarro, '¡Qué cavallo traes, castellano!'
Dixo Rodrigo de Bivar, '¿Quieres trocarlo?
Cámbialo comigo si el tuyo es más flaco.'   685

Allí dixo el conde, 'Non me sería dado.'
Partiéronles el sol e los fieles commo de cabo.
Ívanse dar seños golpes e erról' el conde navarro.
Non lo erró Rodrigo de Bivar,
un golpe le fue dar que le abatió del cavallo,   690
en ante que el conde se levantase, deçendió a degollarlo.
D'esta guissa ganó a Calahorra Rodrigo el castellano,
por el buen rey don Fernando.

El día de Santa Cruz de mayo,
que Atiença avía por reinado,   695
el rey moro Jesías de Guadalajara, que a África ovo poblado,
aquel moro Jessías, mucho honrado madriano.
E sópolo el rey moro Burgos de Ayllón muy lozano,
e vínose para Castilla, de día e de noche andando.
A Bivar enbió el mandado,   700
e quando lo sopo Rodrigo cavalgó muy privado,
entre día e noche a Çamora es llegado.
Al rey se omilló e nol' bessó la mano,
dixo, 'Rey, mucho me plaze porque non só tu vassallo.
Rey, fasta que non te armasses non devías tener reinado,   705
ca non esperas palmada de moro nin de cristiano,
mas ve velar al padrón de Santiago.
Quando oyeres la missa, ármate con tu mano,
e tú te çiñe la espada con tu mano,
e tú deçiñe commo de cabo,   710
e tú te sey el padrino, e tú te sey el afijado,
e llámate cavallero del padrón de Santiago,
e serías tú mi señor, e mandarías el tu reinado.'
Essas horas dixo el rey, en tanto fue acordado,
'Non ha cossa, Rodrigo, que non faga por te non salir de mandado.'   715
Metiéronse a los caminos, passól' Rodrigo a Malgrado,
que dizen Benavente, según dize en el romançe,
passólo a Astorga e metiólo a Monte Iraglo.
De allí se tornó Rodrigo, que le apresurava el mandado,
que se aguissavan paganos para correr el reinado.   720
De noche llegó Rodrigo a Bivar.
Dava su apellido, que non lo entendiessen los que vendían el
   reinado.
A Sant Estevan fue Diego Laínez llegado,

e don Ruy Laínez de Alfaro,
e don Laín Laínez que ovo a Treviño conprado,   725
e Fernand Laínez de Sant Estevan muy lozano.
El alvor quería quebrar, e aún el día non era claro,
quando assomavan los çinco reys moros por el llano,
por la defesa de Sant Estevan, a Duero non son llegados.
Allí aderezó Rodrigo, sus gentes acaudellando,   730
buelven la batalla, llegar querrán al quarto.
Muchas gentes se perdieron de moros e de cristianos, ¡Malos
    pecados!
Ý morieron quatro fijos de Laín Calvo,
muchos buenos cavalleros en derredor Rodrigo los ovo encontrados.
Desque vio el padre e los tíos muertos, ovo la color mudado.   735
Quisieran arramar los cristianos, Rodrigo ovo el escudo enbraçado,
por tornar los cristianos, del padre non ovo cuidado.
Allí fue mezclada la batalla e el torneo abivado,
paradas fueron las azes e el torneo mezclado.
Allí llamó Rodrigo a Santiago, fijo del Zebedeo,   740
non fue tan bueno de armas Judas el Macabeo,
nin Archil, Nicanor nin el rey Tholomeo.
Cansados fueron de lidiar e fartos de tornear,
tres días estido en pesso la fazienda de Rodrigo de Bivar,
a pocas que lo non tomaron entrega, armado estando.   745
Esto le aconsejó por el buen rey don Fernando,
quando los condes vendieron el reinado.
La batalla vençió Rodrigo, por ende sea Dios loado.
Mató al rey Garay, moro de Atiença,
e al rey de Çigüenza, su hermano,   750
e mató al de Guadalajara, e prisso al madriano,
e al talaverano e a otros moros afartos.
Ca muy bien le ayudó el rey moro Burgos de Ayllón loçano,
que era su vassallo.
E traxieron los dos reys moros para el pueblo çamorano.   755
Tornósse Rodrigo para Castilla, tan sañudo e tan irado,
toda la tierra tembrava con el castellano.
Fue destroir a Redezilla e quemar a Bilforado,
conbatieron a Grañón e prisso al conde don Garçi Fernández con su
    mano.
Por Villafranca de Montes d'Oca le levava apressionado,   760
e violo el conde don Ximeno Sánchez de Burueva, su hermano,

e quando lo vio Rodrigo, luego le salió al alcançe.
Ençerrólo en Siete Barrios, que es Birviesca llamado,
en Santa María la Antigua se ençerró el conde lozano.
Conbatiólo Rodrigo, amidos que non de grado,   765
ovo de ronper la iglesia e entró en ella privado,
sacólo por las barvas al conde de tras el altar con su mano,
e díxol', 'Sal acá, alevoso, e ve vender a cristianismo,
e a moros e matar a tu señor honrado.'
Dos condes lieva pressos Rodrigo, a Carrión fue llegado.   770
Quando lo sopieron los condes de Carrión e de Castilla, todos se
    alegraron,
e fezieron la jura en las manos e omenaje le otorgaron,
que a treinta días contados fuessen ante'l rey don Fernando.
Con los pressos fue Rodrigo al pueblo çamorano,
e metiólos en pressión con los moros, e cavalgó privado.   775
E sale a reçebir a los caminos al buen rey don Fernando,
e encontrólo entre Çamora e Benavente, do es Moreruela poblado,
desde allí fasta Çamora fuégelo contando.
El rey, quando lo oyó, enbió por todos sus reinados,
portogalesses e galizianos, leonesses e asturianos,   780
e Estremadura con castellanos.
E allí los mandó el rey tan aína judgarlos,
condes que tal cossa fazían, ¿qué muerte merecían?
Judgaron portogalesses a bueltas con gallizianos,
dieron por juizio que fuesen despeñados.   785
Judgaron leonesses con asturianos,
dieron por juizio que fuessen arrastrados.
Judgaron castellanos a buelta con estremadanes,
e dieron por juizio que fuessen quemados.

Fijos fueron del conde don Pedro del Canpó, mucho onrado.   790
Quando sopieron que Rodrigo de los reinos era echado,
entraron a Palençia por fuerça, que primero era condado,
e a muy grand dessonra echaron fuera al perlado.
E fuesse querellar al pueblo çamorano,
'Señor, miénbresete, ca non te deve ser olvidado,   795
con el rey vuestro padre ove a Palençia franqueado.'
E dixo el rey, 'Muchas cossas que yo non puedo fazer, ¡mal pecado!'
Dixo Bernaldo el perlado, 'Ir quiero a Roma querellarlo.'
Essas horas dixo el rey, 'Commo viéredes más guissado,

ca los reinos tengo que se me alçarán e los fijos dalgo.   800
¡Dios traxiesse a Rodrigo, que sabría caloñarlo!
Ca yo en la romería he abondo, ¡mal pecado!
En la unidat forçada, fasta que yo pueda emendarlo.'

En esta querella llegó otro mandado.
Cartas del rey de Françia e del emperador alemano,   805
cartas del patriarcha e del papa romano,
que diesse tributo España a Françia, desde Aspa fasta en Santiago.
El rey que en España visquiese, siempre se llamasse tributario,
diese fuero e tributo cada año.
Çinco son los reinados de España, assí vinié afirmado,   810
que diessen quinze donçellas vírgines en cada año,
e fuessen fijas dalgo,
e diez cavallos, los mejores del reinado,
e treinta marcos de plata, que despensasen los fijos dalgo,
e azores mudados,   815
e tres falcones, los mejores de los reinados.
E este tributo que diesse cada año en quanto fuessen bivos
      cristianos.
Quando esto oyó el buen rey don Fernando,
batiendo va amas las palmas, las azes quebrantando,
'¡Pecador sin ventura!, ¿a qué tiempo só llegado?   820
Quantos en España visquieron nunca se llamaron tributarios,
a mí veenme niño e sin sesso e vanme soberviando,
más me valdría la muerte que la vida que yo fago.
Agora enbiaré por mis vassallos, que me semeja guissado,
e consejarme he con ellos si seré tributario.'   825
Allí embió por Rodrigo e por todos los fijos dalgo,
enbiara atreguar los condes, que non temiessen de daño.
Llegó con ellos Rodrigo al pueblo çamorano,
e tomólos por las manos e levólos ante'l rey don Fernando,
'Señor, perdona aquestos condes, sin arte e sin engaño.'   830
'Yo los perdono, sin arte e sin engaño,
por non te salir, Rodrigo, de mandado,
que los çinco reys d'España quiero que anden por tu mano.
Ca Françia e Alemaña fázenme tributario,
e el papa de Roma, que debía vedarlo.   835
Vedes aquí su previllegio, con su sello colgado.'
Estonçe dixo Rodrigo, 'Por ende sea Dios loado,

ca vos enbían pedir don, vós devedes otorgarlo.
Aún non vos enbía pedir tributo, mas enbíavos dar algo,
mostrarvos he yo aqueste aver ganarlo.　　　　　　　　　　840
Apellidat vuestros regnos, desde los puertos de Aspa fasta en
　　Santiago,
sobre lo suyo lo ayamos, lo nuestro esté quedado.
Si non llego fasta París non devía ser nado.'
Por esta razón dixieron el buen don Fernando, par fue de emperador.
Mandó a Castilla Vieja e mandó a León,　　　　　　　　845
e mandó a las Esturias fasta en Sant Salvador,
mandó a Galiçia, onde los cavalleros son,
mandó a Portogal, essa tierra jenzor,
e ganó a Cohinbra de moros, pobló a Montemayor,
pobló a Soria, frontera de Aragón,　　　　　　　　　　850
e corrió a Sevilla tres veçes en una sazón,
a dárgela ovieron moros, que quesieron o que non,
e ganó a sant Isidro e adúxolo a León.
Ovo a Navarra en comienda e vínole obedeçer el rey de Aragón.
A pessar de françesses, los puertos de Aspa passó,　　　855
a pessar de reys e de emperadores,
a pessar de romanos, dentro en París entró,
con gentes honradas que de España sacó,
el conde don Ossorio, el amo quel' crió,
e el conde don Martín Gómez, un portogalés de pro,　　860
e el conde don Nuño Núñez, que a Simancas mandó,
y el conde don Ordoño, de Campos el mejor,
e el conde don Fruela, que a Salas mandó,
e el conde don Álvar Rodríguez, que a las Asturias mandó,
e éste pobló a Mondoñedo e den quebrando,　　　　　865
y el conde don Galín Laínez, el bueno de Carrión,
y el conde don Essar, señor de Monçón,
y el conde don Rodrigo, de Cabra señor,
e el conde don Bellar, escogiera el mejor,
e el conde don Ximón Sánchez, de Burueva señor,　　870
e el conde don García de Cabra, de todos el mejor,
e el conde Garçi Fernández el Bueno, Crespo de Grañón,
Almerique de Narbona, qual dizen don Quirón,
con ellos va Rodrigo, de todos el mejor.
Los çinco reys de España todos juntados son,　　　　875
passavan allende Duero, passavan allende Arlanzón.

E siete semanas por cuenta estido el rey don Fernando,
atendiendo batalla en una lid en canpo.
Apellidóse Françia con gentes enderredor,
apellidóse Lonbardía, así commo el agua corre,   880
apellidóse Pavía, e otras gentes,
apellidóse Alemaña con el emperador,
Pulla e Calabra e Sezilla la mayor,
e toda tierra de Roma, con quantas gentes son,
e Armenia e Persia la mayor,   885
e Frandes e Rochella e toda tierra de Ultramar,
e el palazín de Blaya, Saboya la mayor.
Quales atavetradores del buen rey don Fernando,
el conde don Firuela e el conde don Ximón Sánchez,
vieron venir grandes poderes del conde saboyano,   890
con mill e nueveçientos cavalleros a cavallo.
Veniéronse contra el rey de Castilla, llamando,
'¡A las armas, cavalleros, el buen rey don Fernando!
A Ruédano passemos ante que prendamos daño,
que atantos son françesses commo yervas del canpo.'   895
Essas horas dixo el rey don Fernando, 'Non es lo que yo demando.
Grandes tiempos ha passado que yo salí de mis reinados,
quantos d'ella saqué todos son despensados.
El día que yo cobdiçiava ya se me va allegando,
de verme en lid en campo con quien me llama tributario.   900
Varones, ¿qué me fizo rey, señor de España?
La mesura de vosotros, fijos dalgo,
llamástesme señor e bessástesme la mano.
Yo un omne só señero, commo uno de vosotros,
quanto es del mi cuerpo, non puede más que otro omne,   905
mas do yo metier las manos, ¡por Dios, vós sacaldas!,
que grand pressión espera España mientra el mundo fuere.
Que vos non llamen tributarios en ninguna sazón,
ca vos orarían mal sieglo quantos por naçer son.'
A ninguna destas querellas ninguno non le respondió.   910
El rey con la malenconía, por el corazón quería quebrar,
demandó por Rodrigo, el que naçió en Bivar.
Recudióle Rodrigo, la mano le bessó,
'¿Qué vos plaze, señor, el buen rey don Fernando?
Si conde o rico omne vos salió de mandado,   915
muerto o presso metérvoslo he en vuestra mano.'

Essas oras dixo el rey, 'Seyas bienaventurado,
mas sey alferze de mi seña, siempre te lo avré en grado,
e si me Dios torna a España, siempre te faré algo.'
Allí dixo Rodrigo, 'Señor, non me sería dado,   920
do está tanto omne rico e tanto conde e tanto poderosso fijo de algo,
a quien perteneçe seña de señor tan honrado,
e yo só escudero e non cavallero armado.
Mas besso vuestras manos e pídovos un don,
que los primeros golpes yo con mis manos los tome,   925
e abrirvos he los caminos por do entredes vós.'
Essas horas dixo el rey, 'Otórgotelo yo.'
Essas oras Rodrigo a tan apriessa fue armado,
con treçientos cavalleros quel' bessavan la mano,
contra el conde de Saboya salió tan irado.   930
Rodrigo nunca oviera seña nin pendón devissado.
Ronpiendo va un manto que era de sirgo, la peña le tiró privado,
apriessa esto de punta a la meter,
la espada que traía al cuello, tiróla tan privado,
quinze ramos faze la seña.   935
Vergüença avía de la dar a los cavalleros.
E bolvió los ojos en alto,
vio estar un su sobrino, fijo de su hermano,
quel' dizen Pero Mudo, a él fue llegado,
'Ven acá, mi sobrino, fijo eres de mi hermano,   940
el que fizo mi padre en una labradora quando andava cazando.
Varón, toma esta seña, faz lo que yo te mando.'
Dixo Pero Bermudo, 'Que me plaze de grado.
Conosco que só vuestro sobrino, fijo de vuestro hermano,
mas de que saliestes de España, non vos ovo menbrado,   945
a çena nin a yantar non me oviestes conbidado,
de fanbre e de frío só muy coitado.
Non he por cobertura sinon la del cavallo,
por las crietas de los pies córreme sangre clara.'
Allí dixo Rodrigo, 'Calla traidor provado,   950
todo omne de buen logar que quiere sobir a buen estado,
conviene que de lo suyo sea abidado,
que atienda mal e bien sepa el mundo passarlo.'
Pero Mudo tan apriessa fue armado,
reçebió la seña, a Rodrigo bessó la mano,   955
e dixo, 'Señor, afruenta de Dios te fago.

Vey la seña sin arte e sin engaño,
que en tal logar vos la pondré antes del sol çerrado,
do nunca entró seña de moro nin de cristiano.'
Allí dixo Rodrigo, 'Esso es lo que yo te mando.　　　　960
Agora te conosco, que eres fijo de mi hermano.'
Con treçientos cavalleros iva la seña guardando.
Violo el conde de Saboya, en tanto fue espantado,
e dixo a los cavalleros, 'Cavalgat muy privado,
sabedme de aquel español, si viene de la tierra echado.　　　965
Si fuere conde o rico omne, véngame bessar la mano,
si fuere omne de buen logar, tome mio mayoradgo.'
Tan apriessa los latinos a Rodrigo son llegados,
e fízose maravillado quando ge lo contaron,
'Tornatvos,' dixo, 'latinos, al conde con mi mandado,　　　970
e dezilde que non só rico nin poderoso fidalgo.
Mas só un escudero, non cavallero armado,
fijo de un mercadero, nieto de un çibdadano.
Mi padre moró en rúa e siempre vendió su paño,
fincáronme dos pieças el día que fue finado.　　　975
E commo él vendió lo suyo, venderé yo lo mio de grado,
ca quien ge lo conprava múchol' costava caro.
Pero dezilde al conde, que de mi cuerpo atanto,
que de muerto o presso non me saldría de la mano.'
El conde quando esto oyó, fue mucho sañudo e irado,　　　980
'¡Español, fi de enemiga, ya nos viene menazando!
Todos los otros mueran, aquél sea pressionado,
e levátmelo a Saboya, muy las manos atadas.
Colgarlo he de los cabellos, del castillo privado.
Mandaré a mis rapazes tan sin duelo golparlo,　　　985
que en el mediodía diga que es noche çerrada.'
Caudillan las azes e lidian tan de grado.
'¡Saboya!' llamó el conde e '¡Castilla!' el castellano.
Veredes lidiar a porfía e tan firme se dar,
atantos pendones obrados alçar e abaxar,　　　990
atantas lanças quebradas por el primero quebrar,
atantos cavallos caer e non se levantar,
atanto cavallo sin dueño por el campo andar.
En medio de la mayor priessa Rodrigo fue entrar,
encontrósse con el conde, un golpe le fue dar,　　　995
derribólo del cavallo, non le quisso matar.

'Presso sodes, don conde, el onrado saboyano,
d'esta guisa vende paño aqueste çibdadano.
Assí los vendió mi padre fasta que fue finado,
quien ge los conprava, assí les costava caro.'   1000
Essas dixo el conde, 'Messura, español onrado,
que omne que así lidia non devía ser villano,
o eres hermano o primo del buen rey don Fernando.
¿Cómmo dizen el tu nonbre?, sí a Dios ayas pagado.'
Allí dixo Rodrigo, 'Non te será negado.   1005
Rodrigo me llaman aquestos quantos aquí trayo,
fijo só de Diego Laínez e nieto de Laín Calvo.'
Essas oras dixo, '¡Ay, mesquino desaventurado!
Cuidé que lidiava con omne e lidié con un pecado,
que dentro poco ha que fueste nonbrado,   1010
que non te atiende rey moro nin cristiano en el campo,
ca de muerto o de presso non te saldría de la mano.
Oílo contar al rey de Françia e al papa romano,
que nunca te prendiesse omne nado.
Dame de qué guissa podría yo salir de tu pressión, que non fuesse
    dessonrado.   1015
Cassarte ía con una mi fija que yo más amo,
e non he otra fija nin otro fijo que herede el condado.'
Allí dixo Rodrigo, 'Pues enbía por ella muy privado,
si yo d'ella me pagare, que cabe se fará el mercado.'
Ya van por la infanta a poder de cavallo.   1020
Tráenla guarnida, en una silla muy blanca,
de oro el freno, non mejor obrado.
Vestida va la infanta de un baldoque preçiado,
cabellos por las espaldas commo de un oro colado,
ojos prietos commo la mora, el cuerpo bien tajado.   1025
Non ha rey nin emperador que d'ella non fuese pagado.
Quando la vio Rodrigo, tomóla por la mano,
e dixo, 'Conde, it a buena ventura muy privado,
que non cassaría con ella por quanto yo valgo,
ca non me perteneçe fija de conde nin de condado.   1030
El rey don Fernando es por cassar,
a él me la quiero dar, sí faga mayoralgo.
Conde, por quanto de los ojos vedes, non vos coja más en el canpo.'
Dávala Rodrigo a los suyos, liévanla passo.
Él acogiesse para el rey al galope del cavallo,   1035

dixo, '¡Albriçias, señor, que vos trayo buen mandado!
En mill e noueçientos cavalleros fize muy grand daño,
prisse al conde de Saboya por la barba, sin su grado.
Diome por sí su fija e yo para vós la quiero,
e besso las manos, e vós que me fagades algo.'   1040
Essas oras dixo el rey, 'Sólo non sea penssado,
ca por conquerir reinos vine acá, ca non por fijas dalgo,
ca nós las quesiéramos, en España falláramos afartas.'
Essas oras dixo Rodrigo, 'Señor, fazedlo privado.
¡Enbarraganad a Françia!, sí a Dios ayades pagado.   1045
Suya será la dessonra, irlos hemos denostando,
assí bolveremos con ellos la lid en el campo.'
Essas oras fue el rey ledo e pagado,
e dixo, 'Rodrigo, pues en mill e noveçientos fezistes grand daño,
de los tuyos, ¿quántos te fincaron?, sí a Dios ayas pagado.'   1050
Allí dixo Rodrigo, 'Non vos será negado.
Llevé trezientos cavalleros e traxe quarenta e quatro.'
Quando esto oyó el rey, tomólo por la mano,
al real de castellanos amos a dos entraron.
El rey enbió a dos a dos los cavalleros de mando,   1055
fasta que apartó noveçientos que a Rodrigo bessassen la mano.
Dixieron los noveçientos, 'Por ó Dios sea loado,
con tan onrado señor que nós bessemos la mano.'
De Rodrigo que avía nonbre, Ruy Díaz le llamaron.
Cavalgan estos noveçientos.   1060
A la infanta tomaron entre la tienda del buen rey don Fernando,
con ella fue el rey muy leydo e pagado.
Allí dixo Rodrigo al buen rey don Fernando,
'Cavalguen vuestros reinos e non sean en tardarlo,
yo iré en la delantera con estos noveçientos que yo trayo.   1065
Señor, lleguemos a París, que así lo avré otorgado,
ca aý es el rey de Françia e el emperador alemano,
ý es el patriarcha e el papa romano,
que nos están esperando a que les diéssemos el tributo,
e nós queremos ge lo dar privado.   1070
Que fasta que me vea con ellos, non sería folgado.'
Entran en las armas, comiençan de cavalgar,
la delantera lieva Rodrigo de Bivar,
cavalga en la mañana, al alvorada.
El buen rey don Fernando los poderes juntava.   1075

Ya eran fuera de París assentados,
en tantas tiendas, en tantos ricos estrados.
Allí llegó Rodrigo con tresçientos cavalleros.
Allí se reptan françesses a bueltas con alemanes,
riétanse los françesses con tantos de los romanos. 1080
Allí fabló el conde de Saboya, muy grandes bozes dando,
'¡Quedo,' dixo, 'los reinos, non vos vades coitando!
Aquel español que allí vedes es diablo en todo,
el diablo le dio tantos poderes que assí viene aconpañado.
Con mill que trae mal me ha desbaratado, 1085
e en mill e noveçientos fízome grand daño.
Príssome por la barba, amidos e non de grado.
Allá me tiene una fija, donde soy muy cuitado.'
Allí finca la tienda de Ruy Díaz el Castellano.
En el tendal don Ruy Díaz cavalga apriessa en el su cavallo Bavieca, 1090
el escudo ante pechos, el pendón en la mano.
'Oít,' dixo, 'los noveçientos, veredes lo que fago,
si non diesse con la mano en las puertas de París, non sería folgado.
¡Si podiesse mezclar batalla, el torneo parado,
que cras, quando él llegasse, que nos fallasse lidiando!' 1095
Allí movió Ruy Díaz.
Entre las tiendas de los françesses expoloneó el cavallo,
e ferían los pies e la tierra iva temblando.
En las puertas de París fue ferir con la mano,
a pessar de françesses fue passar commo de cabo. 1100
Parósse ante'l papa, muy quedo estido,
'¿Qué es esso, françesses e papa romano?
Siempre oí dezir que Doze Pares avía en Françia, lidiadores,
¡llamadlos!
Si quesieren lidiar comigo, cavalguen muy privado.'
Fabló el rey de Françia, 'Non es guissado, 1105
non ay de los Doçe Pares que lidiasse, si non con el rey don
Fernando.
Apartat desque veniere el rey de España don Fernando,
e lidiaré con él de grado.'
Allí dixo Ruy Díaz, el buen castellano,
'Rey, vós e los Doze Pares de mí serés buscado.' 1110
Ya se va Ruy Díaz a los sus vassallos.
Dan çevada de día, los sus vassallos son armados.
Todos corren la tierra fasta el sol rayado.

Assomaron los poderes del buen rey don Fernando.
A reçebirlos sale Ruy Díaz e tomó al rey por la mano,   1115
'Adelante,' dixo, 'señor, el buen rey don Fernando,
el más honrado señor que en España fue nado.
Ya querrían aver en graçia los que vos llaman tributario.
Agora sanaré del dolor que andava coitado.
Tan seguro andat por aquí commo si oviésedes entrado.   1120
Yo lidiaré con éstos, estad quedado.'
Allí dixo el rey, 'Ruy Díaz el Castellano,
commo tú ordenares mis reinos, en tanto seré folgado.'
Allí fincó Ruy Díaz la tienda del buen rey don Fernando,
con las suyas cuerdas mezcladas, aderredor de los castellanos,   1125
a buelta con estremadanos,
la costanera aragonesses, navarros, con leonesses, con asturianos,
por mantener la çaga portogalesses con galizianos.
Quando esto vio el papa romano,
dixo, 'Oítme, rey de Françia, el emperador alemano.   1130
Semeja que el rey de España es aquí llegado,
non viene con mengua de coraçón, mas commo rey esforçado.
Agora podredes aver derecho, si podiéremos tomarlo.
Quanto aver sacó de España, todo lo ha despenssado.
Agora ganaré d'él tregua por quatro años, es chico el plazo,   1135
después darle hemos guerra e tomarle hemos el reinado.'
Dixieron los reys, 'Señor, enbiat por él privado.'
Apriessa enbía por el rey el papa romano.
Quando esto oyó el rey don Fernando, armósse él e los fijos dalgo.
En seños cavallos cavalgan entre el rey e el castellano,   1140
amos lanças en las manos, mano por mano fablando,
aconsejándole Ruy Díaz a guissa de buen fidalgo,
'Señor, en aquesta fabla, sed vós bien acordado,
ellos fablan muy manso e vós fablat muy bravo,
ellos son muy leídos e andarvos han engañando.   1145
Señor, pedildes batalla para cras, en el alvor quebrando.'
El papa quando lo vio venir, en ante fue acordado,
'Oítme,' dixo, 'el buen emperador alemano.
Aqueste rey de España seméjame mucho onrado,
ponet aý una silla a par de vós e cobrilda con este paño.   1150
Quando viéredes que descavalga, levantadvos muy privado,
e prendetlo por las manos e cabe de vós possaldo.
Que sea en par de vós, que me semeja guissado.'

Allí se erzían los poderes de Roma al buen rey don Fernando.
Non sabía quál era el rey nin quál era el castellano,   1155
sinon quando descavalgó el rey, al papa bessó la mano.
E levantósse el emperador e reçebiólos muy de buen grado,
e tómanse por las manos, al estrado van possar.
A los pies del rey se va possar Ruy Díaz el Castellano.
Allí fabló el papa, comenzó a preguntarlo,   1160
'Dígasme, rey de España, sí a Dios ayas pagado,
si quieres ser emperador de España, darte he la corona de grado.'
Allí fabló Ruy Díaz, ante que el rey don Fernando,
'¡Dévos Dios malas graçias, ay, papa romano!
Que por lo por ganar venimos, que non por lo ganado,   1165
ca los çinco reinos de España sin vós lo bessan la mano.
Viene por conquerir el emperio de Alemania, que de derecho ha de
   heredarlo.
Assentósse en la silla, por ende sea Dios loado.
Veré que le dan avantaja de la qual será ossado
conde alemano quel' dé la corona e el blago.'   1170
En tanto se levantó el buen rey don Fernando,
'A treguas venimos, que non por fazer daño.'
'Vós adeliñat, mi señor Ruy Díaz el Castellano.'
Estonçe Ruy Díaz apriessa se fue levantado,
'Oítme,' dixo, 'rey de Françia e enperador alemano,   1175
oítme patriarcha e papa romano.
Enbiástesme pedir tributario,
traérvoslo ha el buen rey don Fernando.
Cras vos entregará en buena lid en el campo,
los marcos quel' pedistes.   1180
Vós, rey de Françia, de mí seredes buscado.
Veré si vos acorrerán los Doze Pares o algún francés loçano.'
Emplaçados fincan para otro día en el campo.
Alegre se va el buen rey don Fernando,
a la su tienda lieva a Ruy Díaz, que non quiere dexarlo.   1185
Allí dixo el rey a Ruy Díaz,
'Fijo eres de Diego Laínez e nieto de Laín Calvo,
cabdiella bien los reinos, desque cantare el gallo.'
Essas oras dixo Ruy Díaz, 'Que me plaze de grado.
Cabdillaré las azes ante del alvor quebrado,   1190
commo estén las azes paradas en ante del sol rayado.'
Apriessa dan çevada e piensan de cavalgar.

Las azes son acabdilladas quando el alvor quiere quebrar.
Mandava Ruy Díaz a los castellanos al buen rey don Fernando
   guardar.
Va Ruy Díaz con los noveçientos, la delantera fue tomar.   1195
Armadas son las azes e el pregón apregonado,
la una e las dos a la terçera llegando.
La infanta de Saboya, fija del conde saboyano,
yazía de parto en la tienda del buen rey don Fernando.
Allí parió un fijo varón, el papa fue tomarlo,   1200
ante que el rey lo sopiesse, fue el infante cristiano.
Padrino fue el rey de Françia e el enperador alemano,
padrino fue un patriarcha e un cardenal onrado.
En las manos del papa el infante fue cristiano.
Allí llegó el buen rey don Fernando.   1205
Quando lo vio el papa, passó el infante a un estrado,
començó de predicar, muy grandes bozes dando,
'Cata,' diz, 'rey de España, cómmo eres bienaventurado,
con tan grand onra, ¡Dios, qué fijo te ha dado!
Miraglo fue de Cristus, el Señor apoderado,   1210
que non quisso que se perdiesse cristianismo desde Roma fasta
   Santiago.
Por amor d'este infante, que Dios te ovo dado,
danos tregua, siquiera por un año.
Allí dixo Ruy Díaz, 'Sol non sea pensado,
salvo si es entrega.'   1215
'Enpero más queremos aplazarlo,
e tal plazo nos dedes que podamos entregarlo,
o morrá este emperador, ol' daremos reinado apartado.'
Dixo el rey don Fernando, 'Dóvos quatro años de plazo.'
Dixo el rey de Françia e el emperador alemano,   1220
'Por amor d'este infante, que es nuestro afijado,
otros quatro anos vos pedimos de plazo.'
Dixo el rey don Fernando, 'Séavos otorgado.
E por amor del patriarcha dóvos otros quatro años,
e por amor del cardenal.'   1225

THE YOUTHFUL DEEDS OF RODRIGO

And the land was left without a lord when King Pelayo died.   1
This King Pelayo had a natural daughter,
and she was married to Count Don Suero de Caso,
and Count Don Suero made in her a son who was called Don
    Alfonso,
and this Don Alfonso was made king of León.   5
And the Castilians lived in hardship,
and they were at war with Navarre and with Aragon,
and with the Moors of San Esteban de Gormaz and of León and of
    Sepúlveda.
And Olmedo was in Moorish hands,
and from there to the borderland that Castile had at Belorado and
    Grañón,   10
and in the other direction Navarre bordered León and Carrión and
    Saldaña.
And since the Castilians went to the king of León's court with their
    daughters and wives,
for this reason they named two judges in Castile,
and when one went to court, the other would defend the land.
Who were these judges?   15
One was Nuño Rasura and the other Laín Calvo.
And why did they call Nuño Rasura by this name?
Because he took from Castile equal measures of wheat,
and offered them to St James so that he would help them against the
    Moors.
And the count was this Nuño Rasura from San Pedro de Arlanza.   20
And this Nuño Rasura had a son who was called Gonzalo Núñez,
and because he was evil and vicious his father wanted to kill him,
and he defected to the Moorish King Guibén, lord of Madrid.
And there he met Doña Aldara Sánchez,
daughter of King Don Sancho Ramírez of Navarre,   25
who was living as a sinful woman among the Moors.
And he asked to marry her, for here they would not allow it,
and he married her and brought her to Castile.
And he made in her three sons,
and the oldest were worthless,   30
and the youngest was Count Fernán González,
who defended Castile for a long time.
And he entered into conflict with King Don Sancho Ordóñez of
    Navarre.

And this King Don Sancho Ordóñez had a meeting with Count
    Fernán González,
in a place called Vañárez.   35
And while the count had safe-conduct, the king captured him by
    deceit,
and took him prisoner to Tudela in Navarre.
And as the count lay in prison, Doña Constanza freed him,
the sister of King Don Sancho Ordóñez.
And as the count lay in irons, the infanta took him on her back,   40
and carried him to a wood.
And they came across an archpriest from there, from Tudela in
    Navarre,
and he said that if the infanta did not make love to him with her
    body, that he would give them up.
And the infanta embraced him,
and as the infanta held him in her embrace, the count approached in
    irons,   45
and killed him with the archpriest's very own dagger.
And as the infanta raised her eyes, she saw great forces coming,
and she said to the count, 'We're dead, oh damnation!,
for behold here the forces of King Don Sancho my brother.'
And the count raised his eyes and made out the forces,   50
and he recognized the forces and was very happy and very pleased,
and he said to the infanta, 'This is Castile, that always kisses my
    hand.'
And the infanta stooped down,
and the count quickly mounted the archpriest's mule,
and on foot went the infanta,   55
and he quickly came out of the wood.
And when the Castilains saw him, they all marvelled,
but they did not kiss his hand nor did they call him lord,
for they had rendered homage to a stone that they brought in a cart,
that they were keeping as their lord until they found the count.   60
And they returned the stone in the likeness of the count to Monte de
    Oca,
back to the place where they had taken it,
and they all kissed the hand of the count as their lord.
And this Count Fernán González, after he took power in Castile,
killed King Don Sancho Ordóñez of Navarre,   65
and beheaded him with with his own hand.

And the count would not be subject to Moors or Christians,
and he sent word to the king of León, son of Don Suero de Caso,
Don Alfonso was his name.
The king sent to enjoin the count,   70
that he come to an assembly, and the count went very happily.
The count rode like such a proud man,
and after a full thirty days the count arrived at the meeting,
and the meeting was in Saldaña.
And he began to question him,   75
'And I am amazed, Count, how you are so daring,
as not to come to my court or kiss my hand,
for Castile was always tributary to León,
for León is a kingdom and Castile is a county.'
Then the count said, 'You are wasting your time,   80
you are on a good stout mule and I am on a good horse.
That I have tolerated you I am quite amazed,
for Castile has a lord and you are asking him for tribute.'
Then the king said, 'In court it will be judged,
whether you should obey me, if not, you shall be free.'   85
Then the count said, 'Let's get there quickly.'
The court is in León, the brave count arrived,
he bears a precious horse and a goshawk in his hand.
And the king bought it from him with wealth in coins,
at thirty-five thousand maravedís the horse and the goshawk were
    valued.   90
At compounding interest the count sold it to him, that he pay it by a
    specific day.
Long periods passed that the count was not paid,
nor did he want to go to court unless it was paid off.
With sons and daughters and wives, the Castilians go to the court of
    León.
And Count Fernán González said this to the king,   95
'King, I will not come to your court without being compensated,
for the payment that you owe me, for my goshawk and my horse.'
When they added up the amount, the king couldn't pay it,
the compounding had so increased that the kingdom would not
    cover it.
The king and the brave count came to an agreement   100
that the king relinquish Castile, the count was very satisfied,
it pleased the count when he heard this decision.

In this way the good Count Fernán González freed Castile,
while at war with Moors and Christians,
in every corner of all his county.   105
The count had a son who was called Garci Fernández.
If the father was a good warrior, the son was his equal.
To the daughter of Almerique of Narbonne Count Garci Fernández
    was married,
and with her he made a son who was called Count Don Sancho.
Seven years later when they killed the infantes of Salas,   110
Count Garci Fernández died, a courtly Castilian noble.
Good Count Don Sancho,
and he conferred on them good grants and good law codes by his
    hand.
And he took to wife the daughter of the king of León, granddaughter
    of Count Don Suero de Caso,
and in her he made a son who was called by name Sancho.   115
So often he went out to the woods as a hunter that he never settled in
    town.
His father gave him the name Sancho Aborter, for his love of killing.
Once his father saw that he was of age, he arrived in Burgos.
Within a full thirty days the Castilians gather there.
Once the count saw them, he rose to his feet,   120
'Hear me, Castilians, I have arrived in a fortunate moment,
to grant you more favour than any born man ever granted you.
Count Fernán González, my grandfather, freed you from paying
    tribute.
Count Garci Fernández, my father,
and I gave you law codes and grants confirmed by my hand.   125
From the county that is Castile, I am making it a kingdom for you.
Let's make my son Sancho Abarca king, if you see that it is
    appropriate.
He is the grandson of the king of León, there is nothing any born
    man can say against him,
that he not be the king of Castile, no one will be so daring,
if not, whoever were to say it I would know well how to stop him.'   130
It greatly pleased the Castilians when they heard this order.
They kiss Sancho Abarca's hands and call out 'Royal, royal!'
throughout Castile they send the news, about the good king they
    chose.
This was the first king that the Castilians had,

with great honour and great riches they had great celebrations. 135
And the good King Sancho Abarca began to reign,
and he ordered his banners flown in every town.
He was betrothed to a daughter of the king of France,
and he gave her to him gladly, they did not do otherwise.
And the infanta is called Doña Isabel, and this was a worthy queen. 140
King Don Sancho Abarca went for her, for it was time to marry her.
To the mountain pass of Aspa they brought her to him, and the king
    of France,
and he went there to receive her.
They have great celebrations in Spain when they saw the king return
    with the queen,
and even greater ones when the Castilians kissed her hand. 145
And Count Don Pedro of Palencia, to Burgos he invited him.
'King Don Sancho Abarca, by all that is holy,
son of Count Don Sancho, my natural lord,
let us go to Palencia, at my invitation,
for I will always serve you as long as my life lasts.' 150
Then said the good king, 'I will do it gladly,
so that in my life you may never be in need.'
This was nine days before the feast of Saint John,
when the King Don Sancho arrived in Palencia to feast.
Wild was the vale of Palencia, for there was no settlement there, 155
except for where they call Santa María la Antigua, where the gallant
    count lived.
They went out to disport, once they had feasted,
and the two crossed the river together.
The king and his mule fell into an underground cave,
the people rush up and took out the king unhurt, 160
the mule broke its forelegs, no born man ever rode it again.
The king raised his eyes and saw in the cave,
a descending stairway of carved stone.
He called for a knight who was named Bernardo,
and says, 'Go, Bernardo, down that stairway and look the cave over.' 165
Said Bernardo, 'Sire, it truly pleases me.'
Bernardo, when he descended, saw a hole dug,
and next to that hole he saw a standing altar,
and above it an inscription, and he began to read it,
he found that Saint Antolin Martyr lay in that place. 170
And he saw a stone with letters and he began to read it,

and he saw that for three hundred years that place had been hidden.
And he came to the king and told him in secret,
'Sire, it seems to me, a holy body lies in this place.'
When the king heard it, he turned to the count,   175
and said, 'Oh, Count Don Pedro, give me this place in trade,
and I will always thank you for as long as I live,
and I will give you for it from Campó all the way to the sea.'
Then Count Don Pedro said to the king, 'It truly pleases me.'
They exchange oaths and the exchange was granted.   180
At that time the count's coat of arms had five stripes,
and two of them were blue and three were of pure gold.
There the count took other colours, the field of pale gold,
a screeching blue eagle in the middle.
They marched along shouting, 'Campó!'   185
That's why they call it Aguilar de Campó, ever since he established
     a county.
The king was filled with joy, happy and pleased.
News reached him of his grandfather the king of León, that he had
     passed away.
He left three daughters and no male son.
For the king was married to one of them,   190
and the Galician Count Don Osorio to another,
the one who made the very honourable Don Ordoño de Campos.
And the other one to Count Nuño Álvarez de Amaya, who held
     Amaya as a county.
And to Don Sancho Abarca were left all the kingdoms in his hand.
And he said to his knight Bernardo that he look after the cave.   195
And you will hear what happened then in that year.
While the archbishop was in the town of Toledo,
on Palm Sunday, at Bisagra celebrating Mass,
at the hour of the Passion, Moors entered the town,
and they captured Toledo, except for the inhabitants,   200
and the archbishop escaped on horseback.
He arrived in Palencia, where Bernardo is,
Bernardo being his nephew, son of his brother.
When he saw the archbishop, he left the cave,
and went to Dehesa Brava to become a hermit,   205
in a hermitage, for there was another town there.
Miro, when he saw this place, he rode very quickly.
He went to León, to the good King Don Sancho,

weeping from his eyes and kissed his hand,
'Lord King Don Sancho Abarca, by the almighty Father,   210
I lost Toledo, Moors have taken it from me.
Sire, give me Palencia and that cave,
and I will live a life pleasing to God,
from an archbishop that I once was, I will live as a hermit.'
And at that moment the king said, 'It truly pleases me.'   215
Quickly he said, 'My lord, go and grant it to me now.'
And arriving in Palencia he took him by the hand,
'Since I bought it from Count Don Pedro, I give it freely, gladly.
And have them draw up a deed granted with my seal,
from Huerta del Campo, where it's called Oter Redondo,   220
including the Atalaya hills and the Cascajares del Bravo,
and on the other side, the hills that go up to Valrociado.'
Miro the prelate accepts it with pleasure.
And he took the deed from the king and rode very quickly,
and took to the roads, to Rome he arrived.   225
And when he saw the pope, he kissed his foot,
'If you please,' he said, 'sire, you who are in place of Saint Peter
    and Saint Paul.
While I was archbishop of the town of Toledo,
the Moors conquered me, which left me in dire straits.
I came to King Don Sancho Abarca, son of Count Don Sancho,   230
as to a man of good fortune who was born at a good moment.
In the vale of Palencia a cave opened up,
and his mule fell in and he came away unhurt.
Saint Antolin Martyr they found buried there,
immediately the king then bought it from a proud count.   235
When I lost Toledo, the king gave it to me,
behold here the deed, how I bring it signed.'
The pope, when he saw the deed with the full seal,
said, 'He acted as a king of good fortune in exempting such a good
    place.
Let us make an edict thereupon that will please God.   240
Since they gave it to the church, let it be granted from me,
to you, Miro, much-honoured bishop of Palencia.'
When these documents the bishop had taken from the pope,
in short order he returned to Spain.
King Don Sancho Abarca heard this and welcomed him gladly.   245
Arriving at Oter Redondo the king took him by the hand,

until they reached San Antolín the king did not want to leave him.
And he said, 'I exempt it for you just as I gave it to you.
Any son of mine who were to challenge this,
shall bear my curse and no born man shall come to his aid,   250
and whosoever comes to his aid shall be considered a traitor,
and by the church shall be damned and excommunicated,
and I give possession to the church with my hanging seal.'
Because the king was king of León, he abandoned the Castilians,
and you see why, because León was head of the kingdoms.   255
Castile rose up against him, and it lasted a good seventeen years.
The other lineages from which the noblemen came rose up against
    him.
Where are these lineages from? From the other judge Laín Calvo.
Where was this Laín Calvo from? A native of Monte de Oca.
And he came to San Pedro de Cardeña to settle, this Laín Calvo,   260
with four sons that rose to good station.
With six hundred knights they defended Castile.
While at war with Navarre, Ruy Laínez, the oldest, settled Haro.
Galduy Laínez received Mendoza from him and settled Treviño,
while at war with Moors, who took great losses.   265
While San Esteban de Gormaz was held by the Moors, and León on
    the other side,
and Atienza and Sigüenza, whereby the Castilians lived in hardship,
Sepúlveda and Olmedo, under a pagan Moor,
in spite of all these, a son of Laín Calvo,
whom they call Peñaflor, Peñafiel was named for him.   270
While at war with the king of León and with the Leonese,
the youngest of Laín Calvo, whom they called Diego Laínez,
this one held Saldaña as a border outpost a long time ago.
Death came to King Sancho Abarca while the land was in this
    hardship.
Three sons the king left the day he passed away.   275
In Alfonso, the oldest, the Leonese had a king,
and Don García, the middle one, took the throne in Navarre.
They took as their lord Don Fernando, the youngest,
the Castilians kissed his hand, like sons of Laín Calvo.
He made war on his brothers.   280
The Leonese were defeated and they took many losses.
At the boundary markers of Mansilla, where the border stones were
    located,

Don Fernando killed his brother Don Alfonso.
Then León and Galicia all the way to Santiago surrendered to him.
He again made war on Navarre as before,   285
and in Atapuerca he killed his brother Don García.
Navarre then surrendered to him and Aragon on the other side.
From then on he was called lord of Spain all the way to Santiago.
He inquired about Navarre, if there was anyone to inherit it.
The infanta Doña Sancha spoke up, daughter of King Don Sancho,   290
and the governor of Navarre,
and the infante Don Ramiro spoke up, but he was not born of a
    legitimate wife.
But because he was the son of this King Don Sancho,
and so as to not alienate the kingdom, Don Fernando gave it to him.
In this way he pacified his land, he arrived in Zamora,   295
ordering his kingdoms to come to his court within thirty full days.
There came the Leonese with the Galicians and the Asturians,
and the Aragonese came along with the Navarrese.
The last ones were the Castilians and the Estremadurans.
Of the sons of Laín Calvo, all four brothers.   300
Don Ruy Laínez was married to the daughter of Don Gonzalo
    Minayas,
and he made in her Don Diego Ordóñez,
from whom come these that are called from Vizcaya.
Galdín Laínez was married to the daughter of Count Don Rodrigo,
the count of Alba and of Vitoria,   305
and he made in her a son who was called Don Lope,
from whom come these Laínez, of Don Luis Díaz de Mendoza.
The infante Laínez was married to the daughter of Count Don
    Álvaro of Feuza,
and he made in her a son who was called Álvar Fáñez,
from whom come these lineages of Castro.   310
Diego Laínez was married to Doña Teresa Núñez,
daughter of Count Ramón Álvarez of Amaya and granddaughter of
    the king of León,
and he made in her a son who was called the good warrior,
    Ruy Díaz.
There the king rose to his feet.
He took the four sons of Laín Calvo by the hand,   315
he put them on the dais with him,
'Hear me, knights, very good noblemen,

you of the most honourable judge that was born in Castile.
You gave me Castile and you kissed my hand,
with you I conquered the kingdoms of Spain all the way to Santiago.   320
You are elders and I know little of the world.
My body and my power I place in your hands,
that you advise me without trickery and without deceit.
I am the king of Castile and of León, thus I act.
You know that León is the head of all the kingdoms,   325
and that is why I beseech you and I ask you emphatically,
whatever banner you tell me to make, I will gladly make it,
for as long as I am worthy I will not disobey your command.'
The Castilians said, 'You were born at a fortunate moment.
Make one with a gold castle and a blue lion roaring.'   330
It greatly pleased the king when the kingdoms were appeased.
The king governed well his land, like a very experienced king.
He confirmed all the law codes that the king his father had given.
He confirmed the grants given by his grandfather, Count Don
    Sancho.
From Palencia the news arrived there that Bishop Miro was dead.   335
And he gave the bishopric to Bernardo,
and he sent him to Rome to be confirmed,
and he returned a very fine prelate.
And he reconfirmed the grants that King Sancho Abarca had given,
from Huerta del Topo up to Quintanilla and its surroundings,   340
up to Castiel Redondo, where it is called Magaz,
from the other side of the Cascajares hills, where it is called Santo
    Tomé,
up to the other hills that are called Val Royado,
where it's called Val de Pero, which was not settled.
The good King Don Fernando ordered his seal put on the grants.   345

The land was at peace, there was no war in any quarter.
Count Don Gómez de Gormaz did harm to Diego Laínez,
he attacked his shepherds and stole his livestock.
In Vivar arrived Diego Laínez, at the call to arms he came.
He sent for his brothers to join him and he rides swiftly.   350
They raided Gormaz when the sun came up.
They set fire to the outer dwellings and reached the fortifications,
and he takes their vassals and all they have in their hands,
and he takes their livestock, all the ones grazing in the fields,

and he takes to their dishonour the washerwomen washing at the
    water's edge.   355
The count struck out after them with one hundred noble knights,
challenging at the top of his lungs the son of Laín Calvo,
'Set free my washerwomen, you son of the town judge,
you won't face me with equal forces!'
because he is so furious.   360
Ruy Laínez replied, lord that he was of Haro,
'A hundred against a hundred we will be ready for you and in full
    force.'
They swear their oaths, that they would be there on the appointed
    day.
They return some of the washerwomen and vassals,
but they did not give him his livestock,   365
because they wanted to hold it against what the count had carried
    off.
After the full nine days they ride swiftly.
Rodrigo, son of Don Diego and grandson of Laín Calvo,
and grandson of Count Nuño Álvarez of Amaya,
and great grandson of the king of León.   370
He was twelve years old and not yet thirteen,
he had never been in battle, now his heart was bursting.
He is among the hundred warriors, whether his father wanted it or
    not,
and the first blows are struck between him and Count Don Gómez.
The battle lines are set and they begin to fight,   375
Rodrigo killed the count, for he could not delay.
The hundred knights come up and begin to fight,
Rodrigo struck out after them, he gives them no respite.
He captured two sons of the count, much to their great displeasure,
Fernán Gómez and Alfonso Gómez, and brought them to Vivar.   380
The count had three daughters, each one marriageable.
And the first one was Elvira Gómez,
and the middle one Aldonza Gómez,
and the last one Jimena Gómez, the youngest.
When they discovered that their brothers were captives and that their
    father was dead,   385
they put on dark clothes and veils everywhere they go.
Then they used it for mourning, now they wear it for celebrating.
They leave Gormaz and go to Vivar.

Don Diego saw them coming and went out to receive them,
'Where are these sisters from, that come to demand something of
    me?,'   390
'We will tell you, sire, we have no reason to deny it.
We are the daughters of Count Don Gormaz, and you ordered him
    killed,
you captured our brothers and you are holding them here,
and we are women, there is no one to protect us.'
Then Don Diego said, 'You should not blame me,   395
ask Rodrigo for them, if he wants to give them to you,
I swear to Christ, it will not grieve me.'
Rodrigo heard this, he began to speak,
'You did wrong, sire, in denying the truth,
for I will be your son and my mother's son.   400
Think about how the world works, sire, for heaven's sake,
the daughters are not to blame for what their father did.
Give them their brothers, for they need them very much,
you should show restraint with these ladies.'
Then Don Diego said, 'Son, order them released.'   405
They free the brothers, they give them to the ladies.
When they found themselves safely outside, they began to speak.
They set a date of fifteen days later against Rodrigo and his father,
'Let's come and torch them at night in their homes in Vivar.'
Jimena Gómez spoke, the youngest,   410
'Have restraint,' she said, 'brothers, for heaven's sake.
I'll go to Zamora, to plead before King Don Fernando,
and you'll be safer and he'll grant you justice.'
Then Jimena Gómez rode, three maidens go with her,
and additional squires who were to protect her.   415
She arrived in Zamora, where the king's court is,
weeping from her eyes and asking him for mercy,
'King, I am a pitiful lady, have mercy on me,
as a little girl I was orphaned by the countess my mother.
The son of Diego Laínez has wronged me greatly,   420
he captured my brothers and killed my father.
To you who are king I come to plead.
Sire, for mercy's sake, grant me justice.'
This greatly grieved the king and he began to speak,
'My kingdoms are in great turmoil, Castile will rise up against me,   425
and if the Castilians rise up against me, they will do me great harm.'

When Jimena Gómez heard this, she kissed his hands,
'If you please,' she said, 'sire, do not take it badly,
I'll show you how to pacify Castile, and your kingdoms as well.
Give me Rodrigo as my husband, the one who killed my father.'   430
When Count Don Osorio heard this, tutor to King Don Fernando,
he took the king by the hand and drew him aside,
'Sire, what do you think? What a gift she has requested of you!
You should truly thank the almighty Father.
Sire, send for Rodrigo and for his father immediately.'   435
They prepare the letters hurriedly, they do not want to delay.
They give them to the messenger, he has taken to the road.
When he arrived in Vivar, Don Diego was resting.
He said, 'I bow to you, sire, for I bring you good news,
good king Don Fernando sends for you and for your son.   440
See here his signed letters that I bring you,
for if God wills it Rodrigo will soon attain eminence.'
Don Diego looked over the letters and his colour changed,
he suspected that for the death of the count the king wanted to kill
     him.
'Hear me,' he said, 'my son, take a look at this,   445
I am fearful of these letters that are full of lies,
for in these matters kings have very evil ways.
Any king you serve, serve him without trickery,
and be wary of him as of a mortal enemy.
Son, you go to Haro, where your Uncle Ruy Laínez is,   450
and I will go to the court where the good king is,
and if by chance the king kills me,
you and your uncles will be able to avenge me.'
Then Rodrigo said, 'That is not going to happen,
whatever you go through, I want to go through it too.   455
Although you are my father, I want to advise you.
Take all three hundred knights with you,
at the entrance to Zamora, sire, give them to me.'
Then Don Diego said, 'Then let us ride.'
They take to the road, to Zamora they go.   460
At the entrance to Zamora, there where the Duero passes,
the three hundred arm themselves and Rodrigo does the same.
Once Rodrigo saw them armed, he began to speak,
'Hear me,' he said, 'friends, relatives, and vassals of my father.
Protect your lord without deceit and without trickery.   465

If you see that the constable wants to capture him, kill him immediately.
May the king have as dark a day as the others that are there.
They can't call you traitors because you kill the king,
for we are not his vassals, and may God not will it.
For the king would be more of a traitor if he were to kill my father   470
because I killed my enemy in fair battle on the field.'
He moves angrily toward the court of the good king Don Fernando,
they all say, 'Behold him who killed the gallant count.'
When Rodrigo turned his eyes toward them, they all scattered.
They all felt great fear of him, and great terror.   475
Don Diego Laínez approached the king to kiss his hand.
When Rodrigo saw this he did not want to kiss his hand.
Rodrigo knelt down to kiss his hand,
he wore a long sword, the king was badly frightened,
shouting loudly he said, 'Get that devil away from me!'   480
Then Don Rodrigo said, 'I would rather a nail,
than for you to be my lord, or I your vassal.
Because my father kissed your hand, I am badly shamed.'
Then the king said to Count Don Osorio, his tutor,
'Get that maiden over here, we will betroth this spirited lad.'   485
Don Diego still did not believe it, he was so frightened.
The maiden came out and the count brings her by the hand.
She raised her eyes and began to look Rodrigo over,
she said, 'Sire, many thanks, for this is the count that I want.'
There they betrothed Doña Jimena Gómez to Rodrigo the Castilian.   490
Rodrigo responded very angrily to the Castilian king,
'Sire, you betrothed me more to my displeasure than to my liking,
but to Christ I promise that I will not kiss your hand,
nor will I lie with her in the countryside or in town,
until I win five battles in fair combat on the field.'   495
When the king heard this he was amazed,
he said, 'This is not a man, he has the look of a devil.'
Said Count Don Osorio, 'I'll show you soon.
When the Moors raid Castile, let no man come to his aid,
we'll see if he says it truthfully or if he is bluffing.'   500
Then father and son bid farewell, they took to the road.
He went to Vivar, to San Pedro de Cardeña, to spend the summer there.

The very bold Moor Burgos of Ayllón went on a raid,
and the very honourable ruler Bulcor of Sepúlveda,

and his brother Tosios, the very rich and very prosperous ruler of
    Olmedo.   505
In all there were five thousand Moors on horseback.
And they raided Castile and reached Belorado,
and they torched Redecilla and Grañón from end to end.
To Rodrigo came the call to arms when he was asleep at siesta time.
He forbade anyone from waking his father, under any circumstances.   510
They put on their armor and ride swiftly.
Three hundred of his father's knights go under his command,
and other people from Castile that were joining with him.
And the Moors came plundering the land and doing much harm,
they brought a great force, with stolen livestock,   515
and Christian captives, oh damnation!
In Nava del Grillo, at a place called Lerma,
there Rodrigo caught up with them, he followed them in pursuit.
He fought with the raiders, and not with those who drove the
    livestock,
and some he killed and the others he scattered.   520
Through the fields of Gomiel they reached Yoda,
where the forces were passing with all their loot.
There Rodrigo fought with them a good battle on the field,
a day and a night, until the next midday,
and the battle was in the balance and the fray was mighty.   525
Rodrigo won the battle, God be praised!
As far as Peña Falcón, at a place called Peñafiel,
they muddied the waters of the Duero as they went.
There they fought a skirmish as they approached Fuentedueña.
Rodrigo killed the two rulers and captured the bold Moor Burgos.   530
And he brought the pagans to Tudela de Duero, and the livestock,
men and women captives the Castilian brought them.
The messengers arrived in Zamora,
where the good king Don Fernando was.
The king was happy and pleased when he heard the news.   535
Oh God, what great joy the Castilan king showed!
The good king rode, with him many counts and knights and other
    noblemen.
He went to Tudela de Duero, where the livestock was grazing.
When Rodrigo saw him coming, he welcomed him immediately,
'See,' he said, 'good king, what I bring you, even though I'm not
    your vassal.   540

Of the five battles that I promised you the day you had me betrothed,
I have won the first, I will account for the other four.'
At that moment the good king said, 'May you be forgiven for
  everything,
provided you give me the fifth of all you have won here.'
Then Rodrigo said, 'Let it not even be considered,   545
  for I'll give it to the poor, for they have suffered a great deal.
I'll give the tithers their portion, for I don't want to be in sin.
From my portion I will give salaries to those who supported me.'
At that moment the good king said, 'Give me that brazen Moor.'
Then Rodrigo said, 'Let it not even be considered,   550
not for all that I am worth,
for among noblemen, when one captures another, he should not
  dishonour him.
I will give you nor more than the fifth of the wealth here in coins,
for I will give it to my vassals, who have endured a great deal.'
They bid farewell to the king and kissed his hand.   555
There were three hundred knights in all gathered together there.
When Rodrigo saw this, he immediately turned to the Moors,
'Hear me, very bold Moorish King Burgos of Ayllón.
I would not capture a king, nor would it be appropriate for me,
but I entreated you to come with me, you did it gladly.   560
Go to your kingdom safe and secure,
and in all my lifetime may you fear no Christian or Moorish king.
Everything the rulers that I killed had, you take it,
if they are willing to open the villages for you, if not, send me a
  messenger,
I will make sure they open them for you out of fear, if not willingly.' 565
When the very bold Moorish King Burgos of Ayllón saw this,
he fell to his knees before Rodrigo and kissed his hand,
speaking from his mouth, 'I call you my lord, I am your vassal,
and I'll give you the fifth of my wealth and your tribute every year.'
The Moor goes away happy, happy returned the Castilian.   570
The very bold Moorish king of Ayllón sent him tribute,
such that within four years he would be rich and prosperous.

Count Don Martín González of Navarre found out, he rode very swiftly,
and he went to the king, 'Sire, feel this grievous loss of yours.
The good king Don Fernando has taken from you Calahorra and
  Tudela.   575

Sire, give me your commission and I will go challenge him,
I will be your combatant, I will defeat him swiftly.'
Then the king said, 'Be it granted you.'
They give the papers to the count, he has taken to the road,
he arrived in Zamora, to the good king Don Fernando.   580
He passed through the court, he kissed the good king's hand,
and said, 'Hear me, king of great power, may I be briefly heard,
a messenger with papers should not take injury or receive harm.
The king of Aragon sends you this challenge, against you and all
    your kingdom,
see here his commission, I bring you the message.   585
Or else, give me one combatant from all your kingdom,
I will fight for the king of Aragon, for I am his vassal.'
When the king heard this, he rose to his feet,
and said, 'This should grieve God and all his kingdom,
for a king to start such a thing when he should be a vassal.   590
Who counselled him in this? And how did he dare?
Who from my kingdoms shall it be, friend or relative or vassal,
who is willing to take up this challenge for me?'
Rodrigo, three days later has arrived in Zamora.
He saw the king was very sad, he stood before him,   595
he was smiling and speaking from his mouth,
'The king who rules Castile and León should not be discouraged.
King, who grieved you and how did he dare?
He shall not escape capture or death by your hand.'
Then the king said, 'May you have good fortune,   600
I truly thank God to see that you have arrived here.
I'll tell you my problem, the cause of my trouble.
The king of Aragon challenged me and I did nothing to provoke it,
he told me to give him Calahorra, reluctantly or willingly,
or else that I designate one combatant from all my kingdom.   605
I pleaded in my court to all the noblemen,
not a single man responded to the challenge.
You respond, Rodrigo, my relative and my vassal,
you are the son of Diego Laínez and grandson of Laín Calvo.'
Then Rodrigo said, 'Sire, it truly pleases me.   610
Give us a grace period such that I may return in time,
for I want to go in pilgrimage to the patron of Santiago,
and to Santa María de Rocamadour, if God will so dispose.'
Then the king said, 'Thirty days will be enough for you.'

The count with great energy rose to his feet,   615
and said, 'King, thirty days is much too long a grace period,
for I would rather face Rodrigo than for someone to give me a
    county.'
Then Rodrigo said, 'Count, why do you complain so much?
For someone whom devils are going to carry off, the long afternoons
    of May are short.'
Then the king said, 'Be on your way, fortunate one.'   620
Rodrigo took to the roads, he passed Malgrado,
which is called Benavente, as they say in that story,
and he passed Astorga and arrived at Monte Irago.
He completed his pilgrimage, and returned through San Salvador de
    Oviedo,
to see the countess Doña Teresa Núñez, and he urgently asked,   625
'Madam, how many days has it been since I left on pilgrimage to
    Santiago?'
And the countess said, 'Today makes twenty-six days,
tomorrow will begin the twenty-seventh day.'
When Rodrigo heard this he was badly distressed,
and said, 'Ride my knights and don't delay,   630
let us go to serve the good king Don Fernando,
for there are three days, no more, before the grace period ends.'
Rodrigo took to the roads with three hundred noblemen.
At the Cascajar ford, where the Duero splits,
it was a fiercely cold day, upon arriving in the late afternoon.   635
On the shore of the ford, there was a pitiful leper,
asking for mercy from all, to be taken across the ford.
All the knights spat and moved to get away from him.
Rodrigo felt sorry for him and took him by the hand,
under a green rain cape he took him across the ford,   640
on a riding mule that his father had given him.
And he went toward Grijalba, to a place called Cerrato,
under some cavernous rocks, where the settlement was.
Under the green rain cape, the Castilian and the leper took shelter,
and while he was sleeping, the leper spoke in his ear,   645
'Are you sleeping, Rodrigo de Vivar? It is time for you to awaken,
I am a messenger of Christ, I am not a leper.
I am Saint Lazarus, God sent me to you,
to blow a breath of air on your back, for a fever to come over you,
and once you sense this fever, you should remember,   650

that anything you undertake, you will be able to finish with your
    own hands.'
He blew a breath of air on his back that passed into his chest,
Rodrigo awoke and was very badly frightened,
he looked all around and could not find the leper,
he remembered that dream and rode off quickly.   655
He went toward Calahorra, riding by day and by night.
There was King Don Ramiro of Aragon,
there was King Don Fernando,
there was King Don Ordoño of Navarre.
The end of the grace period had come and the Castilian did not appear.   660
The king found himself in a bind, and sought out Diego Laínez,
'Diego Laínez, you fight this duel to absolve your son, for it is your
    duty.'
Said Diego Laínez, 'Sire, it truly pleases me.'
Very hurriedly they arm his body and his horse,
when he was ready to mount, the Castilian appeared.   665
The king goes out to meet him with many noblemen,
'Come on,' he said to Rodrigo, 'Why are you so late?'
Then Rodrigo said, 'Sire, I should not be blamed,
for until the sun is set the entire day is my grace period.
I will fight on that horse of my father, for mine comes very tired.'   670
Said Diego Laínez, 'Son, it pleases me greatly.'
The king with great pleasure began to arm him.
Said Rodrigo, 'Sire, I should not be blamed.'
Rodrigo was ready to mount, he did not want to delay.
The fever that the leper had mentioned did not come over him,   675
he said to the king, 'Sire, give me a wine sop.'
When he was about to take the sop, the fever came over him,
instead of taking the sop, he took the reins of the horse.
He raised his banner and clasped his shield,
and he went over to where the Navarrese was.   680
The Navarrese called out 'Aragon!' and 'Castile!' the Castilian,
they charged to strike each other, their horses drew near.
The Navarrese count said, 'What a horse you have, Castilian!'
Said Rodrigo of Vivar, 'Do you want to trade?
Trade with me if yours is weaker.'   685
Then the count said, 'It wouldn't be allowed.'
They divided the sun between them and assigned judges as was the
    custom.

They charged to strike each other and the Navarrese count missed.
Rodrigo of Vivar did not miss,
he struck a blow that knocked him from his horse,   690
and before the count got up, he dismounted and beheaded him.
In this way Rodrigo the Castilian won Calahorra,
for the good king Don Fernando.

On Holy Cross Day in May,
the one who had Atienza as his kingdom,   695
the Moorish King Jesías of Guadalajara, who had settled Africa,
and that Moor Jesías, very honourable Madrilenian.
And the very bold Moorish King Burgos of Ayllón found out,
and he came to Castile, riding by day and by night.
To Vivar he sent the message,   700
and when Rodrigo found out he rode very swiftly,
between sunrise and sundown he made his way to Zamora.
He bowed to the king and did not kiss his hand,
he said, 'King, it pleases me greatly that I am not your vassal.
King, until you are knighted you should not have a kingdom,   705
and don't expect to be dubbed by Moor or Christian,
but go to the patron of Santiago to hold vigil.
When you hear Mass, arm yourself with your own hand,
and gird your sword with your own hand,
and ungird it as is the custom,   710
and you be the godfather, and you be the godson,
and call yourself knight of the patron of Santiago,
and you will be my lord, and you will rule your kingdom.'
At that moment the king said, as he was in agreement,
'There is nothing, Rodrigo, that I won't do so as to not disobey your
    command.'   715
They took to the roads, Rodrigo accompanied him past Malgrado,
which they call Benavente, as they say in that story,
he accompanied him past Astorga and took him to Monte Irago.
From there Rodrigo turned back, for he was spurred on by the news,
that pagans were readying themselves to raid the kingdom.   720
At night Rodrigo arrived in Vivar.
He put out his call to arms, that those who were betraying the
    kingdom not be made aware.
In San Esteban Diego Laínez arrived,
and Don Ruy Laínez of Alfaro,

and Don Laín Laínez who had bought Treviño,   725
and the very brave Fernán Laínez of San Esteban.
Dawn was about to break, and the day was still not bright,
when the five Moorish kings appeared on the plain,
across the meadowlands of San Esteban, they have not reached the
    Duero.
There Rodrigo headed, leading his troops,   730
they join battle, they will want to get to the fourth.
Many people were lost among Moors and Christians, damnation!
There died four sons of Laín Calvo,
with many good knights nearby Rodrigo came upon them.
When he saw his father and his uncles dead, his colour changed.   735
The Christians wanted to scatter, Rodrigo clasped his shield,
to rally the Christians, he showed no concern for his father.
Then the battle turned furious and the combat quickened,
the battle lines were set and the fighting began.
Then Rodrigo called on Santiago, son of Zebedee,   740
Judas Macabeus was not so good at arms,
nor Archil, Nicanor, nor King Ptolemy.
They were tired of fighting and spent by combat,
for three days the battle of Rodrigo of Vivar hung in the balance,
they almost forced him to surrender, while still armed.   745
This inclined him toward the good king Don Fernando,
when the counts betrayed the kingdom.
Rodrigo won the battle, for that God be praised.
He killed King Garay, Moor of Atienza,
and the king of Sigüenza, his brother,   750
and he killed the one from Guadalajara, and took prisoner the
    Madrilenian,
and the one from Talavera and plenty of other Moors.
For he was helped a great deal by the the brave Moorish King
    Burgos of Ayllón,
who was his vassal.
And they brought the two Moorish kings to the town of Zamora.   755
Rodrigo returned to Castile so furious and so angry,
all the earth shook with the Castilian.
He destroyed Redecilla and torched Belorado,
they defeated Grañón and he captured Count Don Garci Fernández
    with his own hand.
Through Villafranca de Montes de Oca he led him a prisoner,   760

and Count Don Jimeno Sánchez of Bureva saw him, his brother,
and when Rodrigo saw him, immediately he struck out in pursuit of
    him.
He surrounded him in Siete Barrios, which is called Briviesca,
the brazen count took refuge in Santa María la Antigua.
Rodrigo fought him, reluctantly and not gladly,   765
he broke into the church and entered it quickly,
he pulled the count out by the beard from behind the altar with his
    own hand,
and he said to him, 'Come out here, vile criminal, and go betray
    Christians,
and Moors and kill your honourable lord.'
Rodrigo takes two captured counts, he arrived in Carrión.   770
When the counts of Carrión and of Castile learned of it, they were
    all pleased,
and swore by their hands and solemnly promised him,
that within thirty full days they would be before King Don
    Fernando.
With the prisoners Rodrigo went to Zamora,
and he threw them in prison with the Moors, and rode swiftly.   775
And he sallies out to the roads to receive the good king Don
    Fernando,
and he met him between Zamora and Benavente, where Moreruela
    is settled,
from there to Zamora he was telling it to him.
The king, when he heard it, put the call out to all his kingdoms,
Portuguese and Galicians, Leonese and Asturians,   780
and Estremadurans and Castilians.
And then the king ordered them judged immediately,
counts who did such a thing, what death did they deserve?
The Portuguese deliberated with the Galicians,
they gave as judgment that they be thrown from a cliff.   785
The Leonese deliberated with the Asturians,
they gave as judgement that they be dragged by horses.
The Castilians deliberated with the Estremadurans,
and they gave as judgement that they be burned alive.

They were the sons of Count Don Pedro de Campó, very honourable.   790
When they learned that Rodrigo was exiled from the kingdoms,
they entered Palencia by force, for first it was a county,

and in a very dishonourable way they threw out the prelate.
And he went to Zamora to plead,
'Sire, may you remember, for it should not be forgotten by you,   795
by the king your father I had Palencia granted to me.'
And the king said, 'So many things that I cannot do, damn it all!'
Said Bernaldo the prelate, 'I want to go to Rome to plead for it.'
At that moment the king said, 'As you see most fitting,
for I sense that the kingdoms and the noblemen will rise up against   800
    me.
If only God would bring Rodrigo, he would know how to make them
    pay for this.
For, hell, I have enough just with the pilgrimage!
We must remain united, until I can resolve this.'

In the midst of this plea another message arrived.
Letters from the king of France and from the German emperor,   805
letters from the patriarch and from the Roman pope,
that Spain pay tribute to France, from Aspa as far as Santiago.
Any king living in Spain always be called tributary,
concede this right and pay tribute every year.
Five are the kingdoms of Spain, thus it continued to affirm,   810
that they give fifteen virgin maidens every year,
and they be noblewomen,
and ten horses, the best of the kingdom,
and thirty silver marks, that they be paid by the noblemen,
and moulted goshawks,   815
and three falcons, the best of the kingdoms.
And that this tribute be given every year for as long as Christians
    lived.
When the good king Don Fernando heard this,
he starts slapping with both palms, bruising his face,
'Luckless sinner! How unfortunate can I be?   820
Of all those who lived in Spain none were ever called tributaries,
they see me as young and without sense and keep demeaning me,
death would be better for me than the life that I lead.
I'll send for my vassals now, that seems right,
and decide with them if I'll pay tribute.'   825
Then he sent for Rodrigo and for all the noblemen,
he ordered a truce with the counts, that they fear no harm.
Rodrigo arrived with them to Zamora,

and took them by the hand and led them before King Don Fernando,
'Sire, pardon these counts, without trickery and without deceit.'   830
'I pardon them, without trickery and without deceit,
so as to not disobey, Rodrigo, your command,
for the five kings of Spain I want them to be led by your hand.
For France and Germany are making me a tributary,
and the pope of Rome, who should prohibit it.   835
See here his decree, with his hanging seal.'
Then Rodrigo said, 'Then God be praised,
for they send asking you for a favour, you should grant it.
He is not really asking you for tribute, rather he wants to give you
    riches,
I'll show you how to take this wealth.   840
Call your kingdoms to arms, from the mountain passes of Aspa as
    far as Santiago,
let us take it from them, and leave ours where it is.
If I don't make it to Paris I should not have been born.'
For this reason they said good Don Fernando, he was equal to an
    emperor.
He ruled Old Castile and he ruled León,   845
and he ruled Asturias as far as San Salvador,
he ruled Galicia, where the knights are,
he ruled Portugal, that noble land,
and he took over Coimbra from the Moors, he settled Montemayor,
he settled Soria, on the border with Aragon,   850
and he raided Seville three times in one season,
Moors had to give it to him, whether they liked it or not,
he recovered Saint Isidore and brought him to León.
He held Navarre in regency and the king of Aragon came to obey
    him.
In spite of the French, he traversed the mountain pass of   855
    Aspa,
in spite of kings and of emperors,
in spite of the Romans, he entered Paris,
with honourable people that he brought from Spain,
Count Don Osorio, the tutor who guided him,
and Count Don Martín Gómez, a noble Portuguese,   860
and Count Don Nuño Núñez, who governed Simancas,
and Count Don Ordoño, the best of Campos,
and Count Don Fruela, who governed Salas,

and Count Don Álvar Rodríguez, who governed Asturias,
and this one settled Mondoñedo and from there he fought,   865
and Count Don Galín Laínez, the good one from Carrión,
and Count Don Essar, lord of Monzón,
and Count Don Rodrigo, lord of Cabra,
and Count Don Bellar, he chose the best,
and Count Don Simón Sánchez, lord of Bureba,   870
and Count Don García of Cabra, the best of all,
and Count Garci Fernández the Good, the curly-haired one from
    Grañón,
Almerique of Narbonne, whom they call Don Quirón,
with them goes Rodrigo, the best of all.
The five kings of Spain have all come together,   875
they passed beyond the Duero, they passed beyond the
    Arlanzón.
And for seven weeks in all King Don Fernando stayed,
awaiting battle and a fight on the field.
France rallied to war with her neighbouring peoples,
Lombardy rallied like a rushing stream,   880
Pavia rallied, and other peoples,
Germany rallied behind the emperor,
Apulia and Calabria and Sicily the Greater,
and all the land of Rome with all the people there,
and Armenia and Persia the Greater,   885
and Flanders and La Rochelle and all the lands beyond the
    seas,
and the principality of Blaye, and Savoy the Greater.
As scouts of the good king Don Fernando,
Count Don Fruela and Count Don Simón Sánchez,
they saw coming great forces of the count of Savoy,   890
with a thousand nine hundred knights on horseback.
They came before the king of Castile, calling out,
'To arms, knights, good king Don Fernando!
Let us cross the Rhone before we take losses,
for the French are as numerous as grass in the field.'   895
At that moment King Don Fernando said, 'This is not what I
    demand.
A long time has passed since I left my kingdoms,
all that I took from there has been spent.
The day that I longed for has finally come,

to see myself in combat with the one who calls me tributary.   900
Men, what made me king, lord of Spain?
Your good judgement, you noble men,
you called me lord and kissed my hand.
I am only one man, like any of you,
as far as my body, it can do no more than any another man,   905
but wherever I place my hands, by God, you pull them free!
for Spain will face great danger for as long as the world shall last.
Do not let them call you tributaries even once,
for those who are yet to be born would pray for your eternal
    damnation.'
To none of these entreaties did anyone respond.   910
The king with his melancholy, his heart was ready to break,
he called for Rodrigo, the one who was born in Vivar.
Rodrigo approached him, he kissed his hand,
'What pleases you, sire, the good king Don Fernando?
If a count or baron has disobeyed your command,   915
dead or captive I will place him in your hand.'
At that moment the king said, 'May you have good fortune,
but be the bearer of my banner, I will be forever grateful to you for
    it,
and if God returns me to Spain, I will reward you well.'
Then Rodrigo said, 'Sire, it wouldn't be appropriate,   920
where there are so many barons and so many counts and so many
    powerful noblemen,
to whom befits the banner of such an honourable lord,
and I am a squire and not a knighted warrior.
But I kiss your hands and ask a favour of you,
that the first blows I be allowed to strike them with my own hands,   925
and I will open the way through which you may pass.'
At that moment said the king, 'I so grant it.'
At that moment Rodrigo very hurriedly was armed,
along with three hundred knights who kissed his hand,
against the count of Savoy he set out very angrily.   930
He had never had a banner or an emblazoned pennon.
He began tearing up a mantle made of silk, he quickly ripped out the
    lining,
hurriedly to put the tip to it,
the sword he wore around his neck, he took it out quickly,
he makes the banner of fifteen strips.   935

He was ashamed to give it to his knights.
And he looked up,
he saw a nephew of his standing there, son of his brother,
who is called Pedro the Mute, he approached him,
'Come here, my nephew, you are the son of my brother,   940
the one my father made in a peasant woman when he was out
    hunting.
Young man, take this banner, do as I command you.'
Said Pedro Bermudo, 'It truly pleases me.
I recognize that I am your nephew, son of your brother,
but since you left Spain, you haven't brought it up,   945
to dine or to feast you haven't invited me,
from hunger and from cold I am suffering.
I have no cover but that of my horse,
from the cuts in my feet blood flows freely.'
Then Rodrigo said, 'Be quiet you proven traitor,   950
any well-born man who wants to rise to good station,
best be able to take care of himself,
that he face up to difficulties and know well how to overcome the
    trials of this world.'
Pedro the Mute was armed very hurriedly,
he took the banner, he kissed Rodrigo's hand,   955
and said, 'Sire, I'll make you a sacred pledge.
Watch the banner closely,
for before sunset I'll put it in such a place,
where never before has gone the banner of Moor or Christian.'
Then Rodrigo said, 'That is what I want from you.   960
Now I recognize you, that you are the son of my brother.'
With three hundred knights he went out protecting the banner.
The count of Savoy saw him, and immediately was frightened,
and he said to his knights, 'Ride very swiftly,
find out about that Spaniard for me, if he comes exiled from his
    land.   965
If he is a count or baron, let him come kiss my hand,
if he is a well-born man, let him be my heir.'
Very quickly the Latins approach Rodrigo,
and he acted surprised when they told him,
'Go back,' he said, 'Latins, to the count with my message,   970
and tell him that I am not rich or a powerful nobleman.
But I am a squire, not a knighted warrior,

son of a merchant, grandson of a burgher.
My father lived in town and always sold his cloth,
two pieces were left to me the day he passed away.   975
And as he sold his, I will sell mine gladly,
for whoever bought it from him, it cost him very dearly.
But tell the count that with all my bodily strength,
that dead or captive he will not escape from my hand.'
The count when he heard this, was very furious and angry,   980
'A Spaniard, son of a devil woman, comes to us making threats!
Let all the others die, I want that one captured,
and take him to me in Savoy, his hands well tied.
I'll hang him by his hair from the castle immediately.
I'll order my servant-boys to beat him so mercilessly,   985
that at midday he will swear it is darkest night.'
They draw the battle lines and fight so willingly.
'Savoy!' cried the count and 'Castile,' the Castilian.
You will see them fighting fiercely and striking each with great
     force,
so many sewn pennons rising and falling,   990
so many lances broken at the first breaking,
so many horses falling and not getting up,
so many horses without riders wandering on the battlefield.
Into the middle of the greatest furor Rodrigo headed,
he came upon the count, he struck him a blow,   995
he knocked him off his horse, he decided not to kill him,
'You are captured, Don Count, the honourable Savoyard,
this is how this burgher sells his cloth.
The same way my father sold it until he passed away,
whoever bought it from him paid just as dearly.'   1000
Then said the count, 'Be reasonable, honourable Spaniard,
for any man who fights like that must not be a townsman,
either you are a brother or a cousin of the good king Don Fernando.
What name do they call you? may you please God.'
Then Rodrigo said, 'It will not be denied you.   1005
All these men that I bring here call me Rodrigo,
I am the son of Diego Laínez and grandson of Laín Calvo.'
At that moment he said, 'Oh, unfortunate wretch!
I thought that I was fighting with a man and I fought with a devil,
for just a little while ago you were mentioned,   1010
that no Moorish king or Christian faces you on the field,

for dead or captive they won't escape from your hand.
I heard it said by the king of France and the pope of Rome,
that no born man ever captured you.
Give me a way to be freed from your captivity, without being
    dishonoured.   1015
I will marry you to my daughter, the one that I love most,
and I have no other daughter or son to inherit the county.'
Then said Rodrigo, 'Well, send for her very quickly,
if I am pleased by her, then the deal will be made quickly.'
They now go for the infanta at full gallop.   1020
They bring her dressed, on a snow-white seat,
the reins of gold, none better wrought.
The infanta is dressed in precious brocade,
her hair over her shoulders is like purest gold,
eyes black as the mulberry, her body well sculpted.   1025
There is not a king or emperor who would not be pleased with her.
When Rodrigo saw her he took her by the hand,
and said, 'Count, go in good fortune very quickly,
I would not marry her for all that I am worth,
for neither a count's daughter nor a county is right for me.   1030
King Don Fernando should marry soon,
I want to give her to him, may he make an heir.
Count, for the sake of all that your eyes can see, may I never catch
    you again on the field.'
Rodrigo gave her to his men, they take her at a slow pace.
He headed for the king at full gallop,   1035
he said, 'A reward, sire, for I bring you a good message!
Against a thousand nine hundred knights I caused very great
    destruction,
I captured the count of Savoy by the beard, against his will.
He gave me his daughter in exchange for himself and I want you to
    have her,
and I kiss your hands, that you might reward me.'   1040
At that moment the king said, 'Don't even let it be considered,
for I came here to conquer kingdoms, not for noblewomen,
for if we wanted them, in Spain we would find plenty.'
At that moment Rodrigo said, 'Sire, do it quickly.
Make France your mistress! may you please God.   1045
The dishonour will be theirs, we will keep insulting them,
that's how we will engage them in battle on the field.'

At that moment the king was happy and pleased,
and he said, 'Rodrigo, so against a thousand and nine hundred
   you caused great destruction,
of yours, how many remain? may you please God.'   1050
Then Rodrigo said, 'It will not be denied you.
I took three hundred knights and I brought back forty-four.'
When the king heard this, he took him by the hand,
into the Castilian camp they both went.
The king sent out by twos the knights under his command,   1055
until he had selected nine hundred to kiss Rodrigo's hand.
The nine hundred said, 'For this God be praised,
for such an honourable lord for us to kiss his hand.'
He whose name was Rodrigo, they called him Ruy Díaz.
These nine hundred mount.   1060
They took the infanta into the tent of the good king Don Fernando,
with her the king was happy and pleased.
Then Rodrigo said to the good king Don Fernando,
'Let your kingdoms ride and let them not delay,
I'll go in the vanguard with these nine hundred that I am bringing. 1065
Sire, let's make it to Paris, for thus I'll have it granted,
for there is the king of France and the German emperor,
there is the patriarch and the Roman pope,
they are waiting for us to give them the tribute,
and we want to give it to them soon.   1070
For until I confront them, I won't be satisfied.'
They arm themselves, they begin to ride,
Rodrigo of Vivar leads the vanguard,
he rides in the morning, at dawn.
Good king Don Fernando gathered his forces.   1075
They were now encamped outside Paris,
in so many tents, on so many rich daises.
There Rodrigo arrived with three hundred knights.
There the French together with the Germans are challenged,
the French together with so many Romans are challenged.   1080
There spoke the count of Savoy, shouting with a very loud voice,
'Steady,' he said, 'you kingdoms, don't get worked up!
That Spaniard that you see there is a devil in every way,
the Devil gave him so many forces so that he comes accompanied
   like that.
With one thousand men that he brings, he routed me badly,   1085

and against a thousand nine hundred he did me great harm.
He grabbed me by the beard, against my will and not to my liking.
He has a daughter of mine over there, which pains me greatly.'
There Ruy Díaz the Castilian pitches his tent.
In the enclosure, Don Ruy Díaz quickly mounts his horse Babieca,   1090
his shield before his chest, his pennon in his hand.
'Listen,' he said, 'you nine hundred, you will see what I do,
if I do not strike the gates of Paris with my hand, I will not rest.
If I could engage them in battle, the encounter launched,
then tomorrow, when he arrives, he would find us fighting.'   1095
Then Ruy Díaz set out.
Through the tents of the French he spurred his horse,
and the hooves struck and the ground was shaking.
The gates of Paris he struck with his hand,
in spite of the French, he got through as before.   1100
He stopped before the pope, he stood very still,
'What is wrong, Frenchmen and Roman Pope?
I always heard that France had twelve peers, fighters, call them!
If they want to fight me, have them mount immediately.'
The king of France spoke, 'It is not appropriate,   1105
none of the twelve peers will fight unless it is with the king Don
    Fernando.
Step aside until the king of Spain Don Fernando comes,
and I'll fight him gladly.'
Then said Ruy Díaz, the good Castilian,
'King, you and the twelve peers will be sought out by me.'   1110
Now Ruy Díaz goes to his vassals.
They feed barley to their horses by day, his vassals are armed.
They raid the land until sunrise.
The forces of the good king Don Fernando appeared.
Ruy Díaz goes out to receive them and he took the king by the hand.   1115
'Come in,' he said, 'sire, good king Don Fernando,
the most honourable lord that in Spain was born.
They so wish to be in your grace those who call you tributary.
Now I will heal from the pain that was troubling me.
Feel free to move about here as if you were indoors.   1120
I'll fight with them, you stay here resting.'
Then the king said, 'Ruy Díaz the Castilian,
as long as you command my kingdoms, I will be at ease.'
There Ruy Díaz pitched the tent of the good king Don Fernando,

the ropes crossed with his own, around him the Castilians,   1125
along with the Estremadurans,
on the flanks Aragonese, Navarrese, with Leonese, with Asturians,
to hold the rear Portuguese and Galicians.
When the Roman pope saw this,
he said, 'Hear me, King of France, German Emperor.   1130
It seems that the king of Spain has arrived here,
he has not come faint of heart, but as a powerful king.
You will be able to claim your rights, if we can capture him.
The wealth he took out of Spain, he has spent it all.
Now I will win from him a four-year truce, it is a short period,   1135
after that we will make war on him and we will take his kingdom.'
The kings said, 'Sire, send for him immediately.'
Hurriedly the Roman pope sends for the king.
When King Don Fernando heard this, he and his noblemen armed
    themselves.
Each on his own horse the king and the Castilian ride together,   1140
both with lance in hand, speaking to each other,
Ruy Díaz counselling him in the manner of a good nobleman,
'Sire, in this negotiation, you must be alert,
they speak very softly so you speak very loudly,
they are well-read and they will be trying to deceive you.   1145
Sire, request battle for tomorrow, at the crack of dawn.'
The pope when he saw him coming, made a sudden decision,
'Hear me,' he said, 'good German Emperor.
This king of Spain seems to me very honourable,
put a chair there next to you and cover it with this cloth.   1150
When you see that he dismounts, stand up very quickly,
and take him by the hands and seat him next to you.
That he be as your equal, that seems appropriate to me.'
Then the Roman dignitaries rose to meet the good king Don
    Fernando.
They did not know which one was the king or which one the
    Castilian,   1155
until the king dismounted, he kissed the pope's hand.
And the emperor rose and welcomed them very warmly,
and they take each other's hands, they go sit on the dais.
At the feet of the king Ruy Díaz the Castilian goes to sit.
Then the pope spoke, he began to ask him,   1160
'Tell me, King of Spain, may you please God,

if you want to be emperor of Spain I will gladly give you the crown.'
Then Ruy Díaz spoke up, before King Don Fernando,
'Cursed be your offer, oh Roman Pope!
We come for what is yet to be won, not for what is already won,   1165
for the five kingdoms of Spain kiss his hand without you.
He comes to conquer the German Empire, which by right he is to
    inherit.
He sat in the chair, for that God be praised.
I will see that they honour him, which will embolden
some German count to give him the crown and the sceptre.'   1170
At that the good king Don Fernando stood up,
'We come for truces, and not to do harm.'
'You go ahead, my lord Ruy Díaz the Castilian.'
Then Ruy Díaz quickly stood up,
'Hear me,' he said, 'King of France and German Emperor,   1175
hear me Patriarch and Roman Pope.
You sent to me demanding tribute,
the good king Don Fernando will bring it to you.
Tomorrow he will turn over to you in a good fight on the battlefield,
the marks you asked of him.   1180
You, King of France, will be sought out by me.
I will see if the twelve peers aid you or any other daring
    Frenchman.'
They agree to meet the next day on the battlefield.
The good king Don Fernando goes away happy,
to his tent he takes Ruy Díaz, he does not want to leave him.   1185
Then the king said to Ruy Díaz,
'You are the son of Diego Laínez and the grandson of Laín Calvo,
have the kingdoms ready by the time the cock crows.'
At that moment Ruy Díaz said, 'It truly pleases me.
I'll take charge of the troops before dawn breaks,   1190
so that they are in formation before sunrise.'
Hurriedly they feed barley to the horses and get ready to mount.
The troops are in formation when dawn is about to break.
Ruy Díaz ordered the Castilians to protect the good king Don
    Fernando.
Ruy Díaz goes with the nine hundred, he led the vanguard.   1195
The troops are armed and the call to battle goes out,
once, twice, and readying for the third.
The infanta of Savoy, daughter of the Savoyard count,

lay in labour in the tent of the good king Don Fernando.
There she gave birth to a male son, the pope picked him up,   1200
before the king knew it, the infante became a Christian.
The godfathers were the king of France and the German emperor,
godfathers were a patriarch and an honourable cardinal.
At the hands of the pope the infante became a Christian.
There arrived the good king Don Fernando.   1205
When the pope saw him, he put the infante on a dais,
he began to preach, speaking in shouts,
'Look,' he says, 'King of Spain, how fortunate you are,
with such great honour, what a son God has given you!
It was a miracle of Christ, the almighty Lord,   1210
who did not want Christendom to be lost from Rome to Santiago.
For the love of this infante that God gave you,
give us a truce, at least for a year.'
Then Ruy Díaz said, 'Don't even let it be considered,
unless it is a surrender.'   1215
'In that case we want to make it longer,
and that you give us a grace period long enough for us to make the
     surrender,
either this emperor will die, or we'll give him a kingdom of his
     own.'
Said the king Don Fernando, 'I'll give you a grace period of four
     years.'
Said the king of France and the German emperor,   1220
'For the love of this infante, who is our godson,
another four years of grace we ask of you.'
Said the king Don Fernando, 'Be it granted to you.
And for the love of the patriarch I give you another four years,
and for the love of the cardinal.'   1225

NOTES TO THE TEXT

The line numbers cited here refer to the lines in this edition, not to those of the manuscript or of any other edition. The manuscript text is presented in two cloumns per folio, which does not allow enough room per line to transcribe complete verses. There are also many lines that are not verses at all, but brief statements or phrases that add to the meaning but have no assonance to mark the end of the line, and are in no real sense poetic. All of this makes the division of lines a fairly subjective exercise, and very unlikely that any two editors will ever agree on a fixed text. I cite Funes's edition because it is the most recent and so available for purchase and consultation, and because Funes cites all precedents in describing his editorial decisions.

1–46 As noted in the introduction, editors present the first folio of the poem as prose, organized into paragraphs. The absence of rhyme indicates that these lines are not verse, but that does not make them prose. Like the verses that will soon appear, they are brief spurts of speech, expressing a small amount of information and joined to subsequent clauses in an adding-on or paratactic style. These lines are not organized by the end-line repetition of assonance, as are the verses that follow, but by the repetition of the conjunction *e(t)* 'and' at the beginning of each line. This structuring device is prevalent in other orally generated narratives, most prominently in the *Iliad*, where the Greek 'step-over conjunction' *dé* 'and' is employed as a boundary marker between one speech unit and another (Bakker 1997, 62–3). It is also common in modern spontaneous speech (Chafe 1980).

48 Assonance begins here, and editors begin to number the lines and present them as verse (Funes 2004, l. 1, p. 7). The manuscript continues to represent the text without acknowledging the paratactic syntax of the lines.

53–6 This four-line passage does not appear to be governed by assonance, but by the repetition of the coordinating conjunction *e(t)*. The transition to verse in line 48 is, therefore, not final. There are also numerous instances in which both assonance and *e(t)* appear to structure lines (ll. 113–15, 136–45, 812–17, etc.).

61 Ms: *a senblança del monte de oca.* Addition of *conde al* completes the sense of the line, based on the narration of the same episode in the *Poema de Fernán González* (López-Guil 2001, esp. strophes 650 and 657, pp. 214–15).

63 The manuscript begins here to present the lines as verses, placing a red calderon at the beginning of every other line. But the clarity in division of lines into verses is short lived, for line 66 begins in the middle of the column. There are additional cases of clear verse division, but the scribe is not consistent in this practice. Further along in the manuscript the calderons are employed intermittently.

66 Funes changes this verse to: *en la Era Degollada, con su mano* (Funes 2004, l. 17). *Era Degollada* is thought to be a place name, although the actual place is unknown. The name is also referenced in *Poema de Fernán González* (López-Guil 2001, l. 306d), and in its prose version in the *Primera crónica general.* Nonetheless, the verse makes good sense without the change, and the word in question is used again the poem (*degollarlo* l. 691).

109 Ms: *Con ella. Et fizo vn fijo.*

112 Funes creates a new first hemistich – *E mandó a castellanos* – to supply what may be a missing half-line (l. 61).

114 Ms: *nuera del conde don suero de casso.* The copyist has made a mistake, at least according to the poem's previous genealogical references (ll. 3 and 68).

116 Ms: *Atanto salio de cazador / quel monte quel non cogia el poblado.*

117 Subsequent references in the poem to this future king of Castile are all *Sancho Avarca*, which have compelled previous editors to change *Sancho Avorta* to *Sancho Avarca, por amor de devisarlo*, 'out of a desire to distinguish him.' The context is well served by letting the verse stand and understanding *Sancho Avorta* as a nickname, 'Sancho the Aborter' [so named] for his love of killing in the hunt. It seems to be an appropriate expression of pride on the part of a father who has big dreams for his son, a future warrior and first king of Castile.

124 This line seems incomplete, although no obvious solution comes to mind.

146–86 This is the first of four passages describing the beginnings and subsequent tribulations of what eventually becomes the bishopric of Palencia. They were most likely inserted into the *Mocedades* narrative with the intention of linking the two stories. If this passage were removed, the line preceding it (145), and the one following (187) combine well enough to support the idea that the Palencia material constitutes an interpolation into a pre-existing written text.

175 Prior to this line, the copyist had written *Quando el rrey. al conde fue tornado*, an unnecessary repetition occuring as one folio ends and another begins (ff. 189v–190r). The line should have been expunctuated, with a dot under each letter to indicate erasure.

190 Ms: *Ca el Rey conla vna fue cassado*. Funes changes this line to '*Ca el conde don Sancho con la una fue cassado*,' a reading verified by recalling lines 114–15. However, the historical wife to Sancho el Mayor of Navarre and mother to Fernando I was not the daughter of the king of France, as Funes would have it, but Doña Mayor, one of Sancho García's (count of Castile, son of Garci Fernández, father of García) three daughters.

192 Ms: *Conla otra. el que don ordoño. / de campos mucho onrrado*. The addition of *fizo* is conjectural.

195 The narrative of the bishopric of Palencia continues here, after only eight lines on the ascension of King Sancho Avarca to the throne of León.

202 Ms: *A porto e Palencia a donde es / ta bernardo*. The copyist mistakes the verb *aportar* 'to arrive' for the city of Porto, Portugal. The copying seems to have been done one or two words at a time, with little regard for context.

207 Ms: *Miro e quando vio este lugar*. The copyist here mistakes the bishop's name for the past tense of the verb *miró* 'to look'. The copyist has transcribed the following: He looked and when he saw this place.

264 Ms: *galduy laynez de se ovo amen / doç a& termjno poblado*. This personage is later called Galdín Laínez (l. 304) and Laín Laínez (l. 725). An additional reference – *el conde Galín Laínez, el bueno de Carrión* (l. 866) – adds further confusion. Funes resolves the discrepancy among the first three in favour of Laín Laínez, since the references to Galduy and Galdín occur in genealogical passages he attributes to a later hand. Funes also replaces the problematic word *termjno* with the place name *treujño*, associated with Laín Laínez (l. 725). I have followed Funes in substituting *Treviño* for *Término*, which is most likely an error made in copying. I have not changed the name of Galduy Laínez, since it is not at all clear that this is a mistake.

305 Ms: *Conel conde de alua & debitoria*.

301–13 This passage is considered an interpolation. Funes removes it from his critical text altogether (p. 31), others place it after line 273 (Alvar and Alvar, l. 225, p. 118).

345 The previous passage is an interpolation related to the bishopric of Palencia (ll. 335–44). In its absence, this line would follow line 334 and close out the episode of the meeting between King Fernando I and the four sons of Laín Calvo. I have placed the line with the Palenica interpolation because that was most likely the intention of the author of the interpolation.

472 Ms: *yrado contrala corte et do / esta el buen Rey don fernando*. Added *va* and removed *et*, following Funes (l. 404), to make the line comprehensible.

503 Ms: *Corryo el moro aburgos / de ayllon muy lozano*. The copyist mistook an unfamiliar given name for that of a familiar town: Burgos. Without correction, the first half of the line would read 'The Moor raided Burgos,' but further reading clarifies the mistake and justifies the correction (l. 530, for example).

565 Funes changes the line to include the oft-repeated phrase *amidos que non de grado* (l. 497), on the assumption that the copyist did not recognize the formulaic expression, as in l. 604, for example. I prefer the original line and the release from repetition that it provides.

607 Ms: *Non me respondio omne nada.* The copyist again changes a formulaic expression common in the poem: *omne nado* (l. 499). I make the same change here as Funes to respect the assonance (l. 539).

615 Ms: *El conde con grand bi- / en pie fue leuantado.* The copyist neglected to complete the word beginning with *bi-*. This speculative addition is meant to provide meaning.

621 Ms: *Alos camjnos entro Rodrigo / pessol & a mal grado.* The copyist misunderstood the entire phrase as a consequence of not recognizing the place name *Malgrado*. A translation of the misunderstanding reads, 'Rodrigo took to the roads, it bothered him a great deal.' When the copyist understood *a mal grado* as an adverb and not the name of a town, the word *passól* became *pessól*.

649 Ms: *que en calentura seas tornado [entrado].* The brackets enclose a copyist correction, written above the line. Funes also accepts the correction (l. 580).

651 Ms: *arrematar las con tu mano.* The transcription is meant to show *arrematar las has,* where *h* is silent and the resulting two a*s* have combined. After the infinitive, the conjugated forms of the verb *haber* 'to have' were employed to form the future tense; *has* is the second person singular of *haber.*

657 Ms: *y era el Rey don rramjro.* Y is not the conjunction 'and,' as in modern Spanish, but the adverb *allí/ahí*, 'there.' Funes also accents the *ý* in order to distinguish it from the unaccented *y*, 'and,' as in ll. 866–8.

661 Ms: *En priessa se vio el & a diego / laynez ovo buscado.* The addition of *rey* completes the sense of the line.

772 Ms: *Et fezieron la jurar enlas / manos & omenaje le otorgar.* The correction is necessary to make sense of the line, following Funes (l. 700).

798 Ms: *Dixo arnaldo el perlado.* Bishop Bernaldo has not died or been replaced, but evidently the copyist is not following the story closely. The correction restores coherence to the narrative.

807 Ms: *Que diessen tributo españa / espa & francia desde aspa.* The story later refers to the demand by France and the other European powers that Spain pay them tribute (ll. 817, 834), and I have corrected this line accordingly.

849 Ms: *jenzor. Et mando acohinbra / de moros.* Copyist error is attributable to the repetition of *mandó* in the previous verses. I have substituted *ganó*, following

Funes (l. 778), a reading supported by the historical conquest of Coimbra by Fernando I in 1064.

862 Ms: *y el conde don ordoño de campos.* Here and in lines 866–8 the conjunction is represented as *y*, not *e.*

865 Funes suspects that this line was once a marginal gloss, later incorporated into the text, and accordingly removes it (see note to his l. 793). The line does break the rythmic quality of the passage, but I prefer to let it stand as testimony to the compositional process employed in the production of the manuscript.

931 Ms: *Rodrigo / nunca viera Seña njn pendon / devissado.* Funes changes the line to '*Rodrigo nunca oviera seña nin pendón devissado*' (1. 858), meaning that Rodrigo had never *had* (oviera) a banner or an emblazoned pennon. Both readings are contradicted by the banner carried into battle by Rodrigo in line 679, although it may be a bit more acceptable to say that Rodrigo had never had a banner (nunca oviera) than to say he had never seen (nunca viera) a banner. This lapse cannot be attributed to the copyist. It is a clear indication of the hybrid nature of the narrative.

941 Ms: *El que fizo mj hermano / en vna labradora / quando andava cazando.* As Funes explains (note to l. 867), this reference to Rodrigo's legendary half-brother reflects a legend documented in medieval chronicles. The mistaken use of *hermano* is attributable to carelessness on the part of the copyist, induced by the repetition of *hermano* in lines 938 and 940.

948 Ms: *Non he por cobertura del cauallo*, 'I have no cover for my horse.' The line as copied diverts attention from the suffering of Pero Mudo to that of his horse, which is bizarre. Correction follows Funes (1. 874).

957 Ms: *te fago. / vey la seña sin engaño.* The remainder of the expression '*sin arte e sin engaño*' was probably left out for lack of space in the manuscript line.

981 Ms: *ya vos viene menazando.* The count of Savoy is not speaking directly to Rodrigo, making the use of *vos* inappropriate. He seems to be speaking to his men and including himself as the recipient of Rodrigo's threats.

985 Ms: *Mandare amjs Rapazes / tan sin duelo. / Que enel medio dia diga / que es noche cerrada.* Something is clearly missing here. *Golparlo* is added as a way to complete the thought.

1013 Ms: *Et al papa de Roma.* This change is meant to accommodate assonance, following Funes (1. 939). Here again the copyist seems more keen on specifying genealogies and titles than on preserving assonance.

1014 Ms: *Que nunca prendes omne nado / Que nunca te prendiesse.* This is a probable scribal error in which the correction '*que nunca te prendiesse*' follows the mistake '*que nunca prendes.*'

1075 Funes adds *ante* to make sense of *juntavan* (ll. 1000–1). I have opted to make the verb singular (*juntava*), which fits the context well.

1076 The forces encamped outside Paris are the Eurpoean powers. The line needs no correction, but could be misunderstood and is another indicator of the sparse expression of the poem.

1078 Rodrigo should have nine hundred men in his army, as in line 1056, and again in 1195.

1090 Ms: *caualga a priessa enl su cauallo / baujeca*. Bavieca was most likely a later addition, retrieved form a marginal gloss, and removed by Funes, as he notes (Funes, note to l. 1015).

1098 Ms: *Expoloneo el cauallo & feryan / los pies enla tierra yua temblando*. The copyist continues to copy word for word without reading the entire line. Without the correction, the line in nonsensical: He spurred his horse and they set their feet on the ground [it was] shaking.

1113 Ms: *todos la tierra fasta el sol rrayado*. I have followed Funes in adding *corren* 'they raid' to give meaning to the line, which otherwise makes no sense. The copyist seems to be in a hurry to complete his task.

1161 Ms: *Digas me Ruy diaz de españa*. The context indicates that the pope is speaking to the king, not to Rodrigo.

1169 This may be the only line in the poem that depends on a subsequent line to complete its meaning.

1173 Although there is no indication of a change in speaker here, this statement should not be attributed to King Fernando, as Funes assumes (l. 1099). It is surely the pope who invites Rodrigo to come forward. This way, the use of *mi señor* in addressing Rodrigo is a little less startling.

1216 Again, here is a new speaker with no introduction, as in line 1173. The speaker is most likely the pope.

COMMENTARY

1 *Pelayo*. The semi-legendary Christian chieftain who, in the eighth century, started the Reconquest, the wars against the Moors, which would eventually end, nearly eight centuries later, with the surrender of the last Moorish kingdom of Granada. Pelayo's first victory was at Covadonga in Asturias, and his descendants became rulers of León, the dominant Christian kingdom in the first centuries of the Reconquest. The text begins with Pelayo to trace the ancestry of its two youthful protagonists Fernando and Rodrigo. Fernando was first count of Castile (1029–65) and later won for himself the kingdom of León (1037–65), while Rodrigo or Ruy Díaz, the youthful hero of this poem, was to be known as the Cid. This first part is obviously not in poetic form, but written as a chronicle or historical summary. The division of the text presented here reflects an apparent structure based on the repetition of *et* 'and' (here reduced to *e*) at the beginning of most lines.

2 *Fija de ganançia*. Historians tell us that Pelayo's daughter Ermisenda married Alfonso, son of Pedro, duke of Cantabria. He then became Alfonso I of Asturias-León (739–57). *Mocedades* takes special pains to emphasize the illegitimacy and waywardness of the offspring of the Castilian ancestry presented here.

4 *Fizo en ella*. This expression sounds very odd today. Christ was 'begotten, not made,' according to the Apostles' Creed, so it does seem appropriate for the Christian culture of the time. It may also reflect the medieval belief that a man's semen was simply deposited in a woman and from the semen alone a child grew. The woman's body nurtured the child during gestation. This belief may help explain the use of patronymics to identify the provenance of an individual.

6 *E los castellanos bevían en premia*. Castile was at first a *condado* or county (realm governed by a count), a 'little corner' of León, with aggressors either Moorish or Christian at most of its borders. The name *Castilla* is from the many fortified sites, not really *castillos* or castles at this early time, which were built as defences.

9 *E era Olmedo de moros.* Either the author assumes that the listener is familiar with the geography of the region and needs no careful explanation of it, or else he is abysmally ignorant of the location of places he names. Evidence from elsewhere in the poem makes the latter possibility look more likely. Naming names, whether accurately or not, was a means of giving authority to a text. Some of the place names appear also in the *Mio Cid*, including San Esteban de Gormaz, where the Cid's daughters are received after their ordeal. In the time of Fernán González (l. 31) it was still in Moorish hands.

12 *E porque los castellanos ivan ...* As subjects of the king of León, the Castilian chief was obliged to attend court in León. So as not to leave the land defenceless when the king held court, two *'alcaldes'* (line 13), known generally as *'los jueces de Castilla,'* were appointed as administrators, and one would stay behind while the other travelled to León. One, Laín Calvo, was a grandfather of Rodrigo in the poem's imaginary genealogy. The other, Nuño Rasura, was grandfather to Fernán González, the first count of Castile and second only to the Cid as a national hero. The poem briefly tells his story as part of the ancestry of Fernando I. After that the Castilians are referred to as sons of Laín Calvo (ll. 258, 279, 300), and later his grandson Rodrigo takes centre stage (l. 368).

17 *¿E por qué ...?* The genealogies of Fernán González and Rodrigo Díaz as descendants of these two Castilian chieftains are included in the earliest chronicles of Christian Spain. Here the narrator anticipates a question about the name Nuño Rasura, probably because it was not a patronymic and sounded strange. Reminiscent of this name, Spanish has *rasar* 'to make even,' and *raso* 'level,' an adjective, but Portuguese still uses *rasoura* 'strickle,' a round stick used to level off grains in a measure. The measure here is *emina*, modern Spanish *hemina*, which in ancient Rome meant half a sextary, or about half a pint English wine measure. Nuño Rasura made an offering of two measures (*eminas*) of wheat to Santiago, St James, the patron saint of the Christian powers in their struggles against the Moors.

31 *E el menor fue el conde Fernand Gonçález.* Epic heroes are sometimes said to have been born in special circumstances, for instance to parents of opposing nationalities. In the popular imagination, they probably need a special origin to match their exceptional character. Here both parents have disreputable pasts: defection to the Moors was a detestable crime. This couple apparently got away with their misdeeds, but would have lived in disgrace after their return to Castile. According to a tradition not mentioned here, Fernán González was abandoned in the woods by his parents, and raised by a hermit.

48 *E dixo al conde.* In the middle of the story of Fernán Gonzàlez and the princess, the text switches from the style of a summary chronicle to the epic form, in the *á-o* assonance, which is used in the greater part of the remaining text. The style continues to be very sketchy, depending on the previous knowledge of the listener to fill in gaps and supply transitions. But the poem does record colourful tales from folklore such as the delivery from prison, the *'mal arcipreste,'* the stone image of the hero, and most of the stories about him that are to follow. These are found in fuller form in the *Fernán González*, a learned composition that is more carefully written but lacks the earthy tone of the *Mocedades*. It relates how the princess was so in love with the hero that she offered to risk death to help him escape from prison on condition that he marry her. Fernán González quickly swears that if she does as promised, he will never marry another.

Though Fernán González was known as a prodigious warrior, in most of this story he does not appear as very heroic. Doña Costanza takes a great risk and shows great initiative in this episode, going against the medieval Spanish ideal of the passive, obedient woman, and her display of physical strength, carrying the man some distance on her back, might be unnerving to most potential husbands.

The archpriest's mule enters the story at a convenient moment, allowing the gentleman to meet his troops mounted, and so with a measure of dignity.

53 *Paró las cuestas.* She crouches down to allow the chained gentleman to use her as a step to climb onto the mule.

58–63 In Montes de Oca, a mountainous corner of eastern Castile, the Castilians had made an oath of allegiance to a stone image of their leader in his absence, and now, in another solemn ceremony in the same place, they recognize his authority.

67 *E non quería obedeçer.* After killing the king of Navarre, Fernân Gonzâlez wanted independence from León.

76 *E yo maravillado me fago.* One of Spain's great folk ballads or *romances* tells this story, with much of the same phraseology as seen here. In the *Mocedades* this episode stands out as exceptionally rhythmical and may have circulated in poetic form, independent of the longer narrative.

81 *E yo sobre buen cavallo.* Fernán González is in battle garb. The king, on a mule, is not. For this reason, apparently, the king makes a concession; the matter will be heard before a court of law.

90 *Maravedís.* A valuable Moorish coin, named for Morabeç, a place in North Africa. Good warhorses and hawks were the warrior's most prized possessions, worth far more than houses or land. By the time of Cervantes, six centuries later, the maravedí was still known, but inflation had made it nearly worthless.

91 *Al gallarín*. The rate of interest was 100% compounded daily, in other words, the price doubled each day, to 70,000, 140,000, etc. After thirty days, the sum would reach 18,790,481,920,000. If the *'largos plazos'* (l. 92) came to half a year, the amount would be truly astronomical.

103 So Fernán González became the first count of Castile (935–70), which he defended and enlarged in several crucial battles. The countship of Castile subsequently became hereditary.

106 Garci Fernández was less successful than his father as count of Castile (970–95), losing territory to the Moors and dying a prisoner of al-Mansur. According to legend he died of wounds after his French wife, Doña Aba, fed his horse nothing but barley to weaken it, so that it fell with its rider during a battle. Doña Aba then offers poison wine to her son, Sancho García, who, suspicious of her motives, forces his mother to drink the poison wine.

109 *Un fijo que dixieron el conde don Sancho*. This son is Sancho García, who succeeded his father Garci Fernández as count of Castile (995–1017). Historically Count Sancho García was a fierce warrior who gained substantial territory from the Moors, and was a constant thorn in the side of his nephew, King Alfonso V of León (999–1028), at times rebelling openly against him.

110 *Los infantes de Salas*. These are the *Siete infantes de Lara* or *Salas* celebrated in an epic tale: seven brothers betrayed by their uncle-by-marriage Ruy Velázquez, who sent them to their deaths against an army of Moors. Their heads were taken to Cordoba as war trophies. At the time, their father, Gonzalo Gustioz, was a prisoner there and was called upon to identify them. In doing so he recalled the good qualities of each of his sons while cleaning the dust and blood from their faces. A similar episode constitutes the only remaining written fragment of a Spanish version of the battle of Rencesvals, glorified in the French *Chanson de Roland*. Known as the *Cantar de Roncesvalles*, it was most likely put to parchment in the early thirteenth century. Only in this Spanish tale are the vanquished knights of France decapitated, their heads retrieved by their king who then laments the loss of each one of his noble warriors. These laments are unforgettable, and that of Gonzalo Gustioz is remembered centuries later in a folk ballad recorded in writing in the sixteenth century. In the epic, Count Garci Fernández is not killed along with the infantes. He is a distant figure of authority not much involved in their affairs.

114 Sancho García did not marry the daughter of the king of León. His son, García, was to be married to the daughter of King Alfonso V of León, Doña Sancha, sister to King Vermudo III (1028–37), a child king of eleven years at the time of this marriage. The young García was assassinated by the Leonese before the marriage could take place, thus ending the legacy of the counts of Castile. *Romanz del infante García* relates this story in two different ways.

115 Count Sancho García had no son named Sancho. His son García succeeded him as count of Castile. On 13 May 1029, as a young count of nineteen years, he was assassinated by the Leonese King Vermudo III, who lured him to his death with the promise of marriage to his sister Doña Sancha and the title of king of Castile.

As the *Mocedades* moves forward, it becomes apparent for two reasons that the Sancho referred to as the son of Count Sancho García is actually Sancho III Garcés el Mayor, king of Navarre (1004–35). First, the historical Sancho el Mayor was the father of Fernando I of León-Castile, the son attributed to Sancho Abarca in the poem. Second, Sancho el Mayor was known to love the hunt, a love reflected in the tale of the discovery of the tomb of Saint Antolín Martyr in *Mocedades*.

116–17 Sancho el Mayor loved the hunt, and for that reason his father named him Sancho Aborta, for his love of killing. This line strikes most editors as odd, so they change *'Sancho Avorta, por amor de destroir'* to *'Sancho Avarca, por amor de devisarlo'* (he called him Sancho Abarca out of a desire to distinguish him). Sancho Aborta is a crude nickname, to be sure, but linked to his love of killing (hunting), and well in tune with the narrative as a whole.

Another reason editors give for changing the name of this Sancho from *Aborta* to *Abarca* is that he appears as *Abarca* in the remainder of the narrative. But this count-become-king is not Sancho Abarca, it is Sancho el Mayor, here nicknamed Sancho Aborta. There seems to be a conflation here of two historical figures, both named Sancho, one who was known to love the hunt, another known as Sancho Abarca.

Sancho Abarca is the name traditionally associated with Sancho II Garcés, king of Navarre (970–94), who had nothing to do with Castilian independence. His son, King García II Sánchez of Navarre (994–1004), was father to Sancho III Garcés, *el Mayor* 'the Great,' of Navarre (1004–35). Sancho el Mayor married Doña Mayor, one of Sancho García's (count of Castile, son of Garci Fernández, father of García) three daughters, and incorporated the county of Castile into the kingdom of Navarre. Upon his death the county of Castile passed to his second son Fernando I in 1035, who subsequently killed his brother-in-law King Vermudo III of León in battle, becoming the first king of León-Castile (1037–65).

127 Sancho Abarca had no role in the history of Castile. *Abarca* is a rough sandal used by peasants in the northeast of Spain. It may refer to the prince's wild youth.

136–45 The assonance shifts to *á*, with much use of the *-ar* of the infinitive.

142 *Los puertos de Aspa.* A principal mountain pass between France and Spain. The Pyrenees are an unusually regular mountain chain, forming a generally solid barrier between the two countries. The pass is symbolic of contact with France; many French pilgrims came through it on their way to the holy shrine of Santiago de Compostela in Galicia, Spain's far northwest, and brought Spain its first significant influence from the Christian outside world.

143 *E él allí fue a tomarla.* King Sancho Abarca went there to receive her. The poem dwells on the coronation and marriage of Sancho to a French princess, perhaps because she is presented here as the first queen of Castile. In any case, she is not the mother of Sancho's son, Fernando. This role is reserved for the historical mother, Doña Mayor (l. 190).

146–86 These lines constitute the first of several episodes related to the diocese of Palencia that seem to interrupt the narrative flow of the poem. Two brief genealogies involving Laín Calvo, the legendary ancestor of the family of Rodrigo Díaz, also seem to have been inserted into the manuscript text. The narrative is entirely coherent without these passages. In fact it reads much better without them, which may be the best evidence that they were added to a version of the *Mocedades* that had already been put to parchment.

This first passage tells of a marvellous discovery near Palencia, a city to the southwest of the Castilian capital of Burgos. The poet's intention was probably to emphasize and magnify the importance of the monastery at that site, as earlier epics were used to advertise monasteries along pilgrim routes and to bring business from travellers, who might stop, spend a night or longer, buy provisions and souvenirs, and hear epic performances. Alan Deyermond has maintained that the entire *Mocedades* was written for this purpose, but Palencia is mentioned only in early sections of the poem (1969, 201).

A similar story is told in the Alfonsine history *Crónica de veinte reyes* (bk. 7, chap. 15, p. 158). Sancho el Mayor is out hunting and chases a wild boar into a cave made into a church, with an altar dedicated to Saint Antolin Martyr. The king wants to kill the boar but his arm is suddenly paralysed, until he prays to Saint Antolin and his arm is freed. This wonder moved king Sancho to resettle the abandoned city of Palencia, to found a church there and to appoint a bishop, and to give the city of Palencia and surrounding towns to the bishop and the church.

The *Crónica de veinte reyes* was written in 1284, and the story incorporated into the *Mocedades* seems to have evolved slightly. But the miraculous nature of the event and the legalistic particulars are maintained in both versions of the tale. The story seems to our sensibilities baldly propagandistic, but the fact that it is included in an Alfonsine history of León-Castile and in the *Mocedades* suggests that the clerics who propagated it were higly influential storytellers.

180 The story tells why the site should always have royal protection and patronage.

185 *Campó.* Campoo, near the north coast.

187–94 In the poem's historical sketch, King Sancho Abarca, as the only male heir, becomes king also of León and Galicia. Here again, the reference to Sancho Abarca should be to Sancho el Mayor of Navarre. The king of León who died during the reign of Sancho el Mayor was Alfosno V (999–1028), who did not leave three daughters and no male heir. Sancho García, count of Castile (995–1017), did leave three daughters upon his death, and one of them in fact married Sancho el Mayor (l. 190). A second daughter married Vermudo III of León (1028–37), and a third daughter married Ramón Berenguer el Curvo, count of Barcelona. Sancho el Mayor managed to wrest the county of Castile from Vermudo III and much of the kingdom of León in 1030, while Vermudo retreated into Galicia in the far west. He also subjected to himself the counts of Ribagorza, Barcelona, and Gascony. So, in a sense, Sancho el Mayor does have *'todos los reinos en su mano'* (l. 194).

195–253 Second passage related to Palencia in which Miro becomes its first bishop.

200 They captured Toledo except for – what? *'Poblado'* could be a mistake of the copyist, or it could mean that the Moors occupied the city, but allowed the inhabitants to continue to live there.

204–6 Bernardo, apparently converted to a holy life in the cave after reading its inscriptions, now leaves to become a hermit at a neighbouring place, Dehesa Brava.

212–14 Miro, the dispossessed archbishop of Toledo, asks the king to grant him permission to live as a hermit in the cave.

220–2 The deed to the property is carefully detailed.

224–53 All this is aimed at establishing most conclusively the church's right to hold this property tax-free and against claims of any future king. At this time the kingship and the church were closely interrelated, but it was not rare for a king to cancel privileges granted by a predecessor to a favoured monastery. Possibly the author aspired to reach the king's ear directly by means of his poem. If so, he surely erred in presenting the negative image of the king that comes later in the work. If not, he certainly intended to shape public opinion.

254–73 This passage brings us back abruptly to the earlier thread of the story and the *Jueces de Castilla*, Nuño Rasura, grandfather of Fernán González and Laín Calvo, called the grandfather of Ruy Díaz – who in history lived a century later than Fernán González.

264 *D'ése ovo a Mendoça.* Galduy received Mendoza from his older brother, apparently.

270 A line or two may have been omitted by the copyist. *Peñafiel* is a place name; *Peñaflor* could be a nickname given to the third son, but he should also have a normal name including Laínez. Later (l. 308) he is called *'el infante Laínez.'*

272 *Diego Laínez*. Father of Ruy Díaz.

275 *Tres fijos*. Once again it is not King Sancho Abarca, but Sancho el Mayor of Navarre who divided his kingdom among his sons. León ascribed to the Visigothic concept of an indivisible monarchy that it had inherited from Roman times. Sancho el Mayor understood the monarchy as patrimony, divisible among progeny, and he was the first Spanish king to divide his kingdom among his sons. He made his first-born son García king of Navarre (1035–54). Fernando was given the new kingdom of Castile (1035–65), and a third son, Ramiro, born of a royal concubine, inherited the new kingdom of Aragon (1035–63), referred to as a 'little fragment' of Sancho's realm by a contemporary chronicler. Sancho el Mayor had ruled over something akin to an empire, *'desde Zamora hasta Barcelona,'* and predictably his sons made war on each other until one had gained all the territory, in this case killing his brothers.

276 Vermudo III resumed sovereignty over León upon the death of Sancho el Mayor, so the Alfonso of the poem is out of place. Vermudo's father, Alfonso V, had been king of León, but died in 1028, before the death of Fernando's father, Sancho el Mayor, in 1035. In any case, Vermudo III was killed in the battle of Tamarón by his brother-in-law Fernando in 1038, who then assumed the throne of León-Castile, styling himself *emperador*, and his wife Sancha, Vermudo's sister, *reina emperatriz*. This is the same Sancha who was betrothed to Castilian count García (note to l. 114).

286 The facts are correct here, occurring on 15 September 1054.

294 Fernando, after killing Ramiro's half-brother, appointed him to be king of Navarre. Presumably the appointee would be loyal to him. Note also that the poem correctly identifies Ramiro as *'non era de velada,'* not born of a legitimate wife (l. 292).

295 Zamora is far to the southwest of León, on the river Duero near modern Portugal.

297–9 The nobles from all over the realm converge on Zamora, demonstrating the king's power.

300–13 This passage identifies the descendants of the sons of Laín Calvo. The action of the poem pauses here, prompting scholars to label the passage a later interpolation. An earlier passage identifies these sons of Laín Calvo, but manages to narrate their deeds as well (ll. 254–73).

The members of the family of Rodrigo are named. All of his aunts by marriage, as well as his mother Teresa Núñez, are daughters of counts, and she is also a descendant of the king of León. Rodrigo's distinguished cousins, including Álvar Fáñez, are also enumerated. The identities here claimed are largely fictional.

314–31 The great assembly of leaders has only one stated order of business. In recognition for the support he has received from the four sons of Laín Calvo, the dominant Castilian nobles, the king asks them to design a banner for the combined five kingdoms, which comprise all of Christian Spain except for Catalonia. Their recommendation, showing the castle and the lion, identified Castile and León as the leading members of the coalition – which nevertheless was to fall apart soon enough. (Though León, the geographic name, and *león*, the 'king of beasts,' are homonyms, the origins of the two words are different. The animal name is basically unchanged from Latin, but the other is from when the Roman Seventh Legion, or army, was retired and settled in western Hispania in the first century. Latin *legio, legionis* developed phonetically into León. Of course, the nobles who took the lion as a symbol of their kingdom were not concerned about word histories.)

335–45 Bernardo, second bishop of Palencia. Comparison of the church lands as described here (ll. 340–4) and in the earlier passage, lines 220–2, shows much imprecision and flexibility. It seems that the author has expanded the area, stressing the continuity of the special exemptions and property rights of the See of Palencia as upheld by the wise new king with the backing of the church in Rome.

346 From here on the poem is more coherent and better written than before, but still with sketchy narrative, crude repetitions and rhymes, and obscure passages, some perhaps due to careles copying.

351 *Quando el sol era rayado*. Not the next morning, as the text seems to say. Gormaz, on the Duero in the extreme south of Castile, is at least two days' journey from Vivar, near Burgos.

354 The cattle-raid was a common form of aggression in early Europe.

355 The women of the town, when out by a stream washing, were not well protected at the time of an attack. Reference here is to the ancient ritual of mass rape that could accompany a conquest, although the text does not specify the nature of the *'deshonra,'* and perhaps it was not assumed to be so grave.

368–70 The lineage claimed for Rodrigo is an invention of the poet based on late tradition.

372 'Bursting' with eagerness for the kill.

384 This is of course Doña Jimena of the *Mio Cid*.

387 *Duelo … gozo*. The line is obviously taken from folk tradition, but the second half is unjustified and perhaps misplaced here, unless it is understood as aside.

392–400 The three sisters consider Don Diego responsible for the death of their father and capture of their brothers (392–3). Don Diego shifts the blame to Rodrigo (395–6), seeming to provoke the son's angry outburst (399–400), although his words, taken from tradition, do not fit the context very well.

401–4 Rodrigo's tone changes abruptly after his harsh words against his father. In line 405 the father still gives responsibility to the son.

419 *Orphanilla*. The Spanish word *huérfano* means a child who has lost either one or both parents, not necessarily both as in English.

424 *Mucho pessó*. The king is faced with a dilemma. If he punishes Rodrigo, the Laínez clan, the most powerful in Castile, will rebel. If he does nothing, he will alienate another powerful clan, appear to show favouritism toward Rodrigo's family, and be seen as a weak and unjust ruler in his other kingdoms.

430 Jimena's request at first seems capricious, absurd, and a betrayal of her family, but on reconsideration it is astute and diplomatic, the perfect solution for an impossible situation. The cultural context should be kept in mind: it was normal for alliances to be formed through marriages arranged by the parents of the bride and groom, and enmities were sometimes solved in this way. Jimena has no parents to make the arrangement for her (though it is true that other relatives could take their place).

432–4 The king's counsellor Osorio is delighted at this unexpected turn of events, which Fernando himself is perhaps too confused and intimidated to appreciate.

445 A change in assonance brings out the gravity of the words of Don Diego.

446–9 This open denunciation of kings, even as spoken by a third person, is remarkable in a fourteenth-century text.

469 *Non somos sus vasallos*. This claim, repeated in line 482 and again later, does not fit well with the text preceding and following. Rodrigo's rebelliousness may be associated with his ongoing initiation (see note to l. 489).

478 The line seems out of place, or changed by mistake by a reviser who was not following the story. Or the contradiction (ll. 477 and 478) may result from an omission by the copyist: a dispute between Rodrigo and his father, for instance, which could also explain why wearing, not drawing, a long sword was frightening to the king. For another explanation of the king's terror, see the note to line 489.

485 Just at this threatening moment, the king has the damsel brought out, seeming to understand that her presence will alter the situation.

489 An appraising look by Jimena at the youth before whose gaze everyone else had recoiled (l. 474) seems to quell his murderous impulses. With no consultation with his father and no forewarning, Rodrigo is betrothed. Remarkably, though his anger continues unabated, he does not refuse the betrothal, only setting conditions for himself: before declaring allegiance to the king and taking Jimena in marriage, he must first win five victories on the field of battle. So, as a great warrior, he will be a loyal subject and a worthy husband. Does it sound like the hero of the *Mio Cid*? If so, as we shall see, he still has a long way to go.

In the *Mio Cid*, line 1333, Minaya Álvar Fáñez, extolling the Cid's deeds before King Alfonso, mentions that he has won *'cinco batallas campales.'* The number does not correspond to battles seen in that poem.

In disregarding the medieval Spanish ideal of the passive, obedient young woman to get the husband she wants, Jimena takes a ròle parallel to that of Doña Constanza, who married Fernán González – but different in that she never loses her femininity. The essential role of the strong, devoted wife in these works should be noted, especially in this age when a good deal of anti-feminist literature was being written.

This story of Rodrigo's first killing and its repercussions may be dismissed as silly and meaningless, the imaginings of an untalented writer. Most critics have in fact taken this view. But the earmarks of the tale are those of a myth of the warrior's initiation – which was widespread in ancient and medieval Europe, including the killing by the child hero, the uncontrollable rage that produces physical transformations (the king twice calls him *pecado* 'a devil,' referring to his appearance) – and makes him invincible but a menace to his own society, finally subdued by a confrontation with the feminine and the controlling power of the eyes. There is also a short sleep, which in this poem is postponed – the order and meaning of the elements is often altered in the adaptations of the myth. The nap is also present in the lion episode of the *Mio Cid*, along with the powerful look and another key element, the immersion, absent in the *Mocedades*. It does seem that the items that reappear would not do so by coincidence, and that they must have been included in the tale of Rodrigo with some form of the ancient, orally transmitted myth in mind. Indeed, in the *Mocedades* the ritual was exceptionally successful, in comparison with other versions that do not turn out well, where the hero ends as a tragic figure.

506 *Moros a cavallo.* There would be a considerably larger number of foot-soldiers, retainers, and others.

510 By not waking his father, Rodrigo may wish to ensure that he alone responds to this aggression by the Moors. If not, the battle would not count among the five he has vowed to win.

543–4 King Fernando, who recently seized most of Christian Spain from his brothers, now appears weak, and Rodrigo makes him look worse by refusing most of his repeated requests for a share of the plunder. This contrast in the character of King Fernando is most evident when comparing the passages that involve Rodrigo with those that do not. When Fernando's deeds are presented in a historical framework – the narration of his accomplishments and of his family line, for instance – his portrayal is of substance and merit. When he is portrayed in relation to Rodrigo, he appears indecisive and ineffective.

This contrast suggests that more than one narrative tradition or source was used to narrate the reign of Fernando I and his relationship to Rodrigo, and that there was little inclination or thought given to modifying those sources for consistency.

547 Christians were required to give a tenth (the tithe) of their income to the church. Rodrigo provides the men's tithes to keep them from falling into a sinful condition.

559 Rodrigo, erroneously called a count in this poem, says only a king, not a count, can capture a king. Still, his deference to royalty does not extend to include his own king. At any rate, in this Moorish ruler he has acquired a valuable ally. In the *Mio Cid*, his valuable Moorish ally was Avengalvón (ibn-Galbun). The Rodrigo of history served three separate Moorish emirs of Zaragoza between 1081 and 1086 as leader of their armies during his exile from Castile: al-Muqtadir, al-Mutamin, and al-Mustain.

568 *El mi señor.* In a ballad, these words are used for Arabic *sidi,* 'my lord,' and thenceforth Rodrigo was known as *(Mio) Cid.* At this solemn moment the Moor uses the *tú* form of address.

575 *Calahora e Tudela.* Two cities not far apart on the river Ebro in Navarre. But the poem says that Rodrigo occupied a place called Tudela de Duero (ll. 531, 538). The matter is unclear; besides, Navarre was supposed to be Fernando's protectorate at the time.

625 *La condessa doña Teresa Núñez.* Rodrigo's mother in the poem.

634 The poem takes Rodrigo far out of his way from Oviedo near the north coast, to Calahorra, by having him cross the Duero, the southern border of León and Castile. *Cascajar* means 'gravel bed.' There are a number of fords so called on the Duero, but the best known is near San Esteban de Gormaz, where several marvellous events were supposed to have occured, including the appearance of the archangel Michael to the Cid in the *Mio Cid* (ll. 404–11). That visitation, like the impending appearance of Saint Lazarus to Rodrigo in the *Mocedades* (l. 648), reassures the Cid that God is with him at all times.

640 *Una capa verde aguadera.* A rain cape became a symbol of the pilgrims to Santiago in Galicia, a rainy region.

648–51 Saint Lazarus is sent to Rodrigo by God to breathe on him. This episode is reminiscent of the Gospel story of John 20: 19–23, when Jesus breathes on the disciples and says, 'As the Father has sent me, so I send you: Receive the Holy Spirit.'

667 Rodrigo de Vivar was known for his habit of being late to appointments. One especially noteworthy example occurs in the *Historia Roderici*, when the Cid misses his meeting with Alfonso VI to relieve the castle of Aledo (chaps. 32–3). This missed appointment angers the king and leads to his second exile.

676 *Una sopa.* A piece of bread dipped in broth or (as here) wine.

679 *El pendón.* The lance with banner attached.

691 Beheading seems a gruesome act to us today, but it apparently was not so conceived in medieval Spain. In the *Mio Cid*, the Cid's daughters beg their husbands to show them mercy by beheading them with their swords instead of beating them to death. If they go through with the beating, the daughters will be considered martyrs and their husbands will be sought out for punishment (ll. 2725–33). Evil protagonists suffer a fate much worse than beheading. Urraca, the instigator of the betrayal against the seven infantes of Salas mentioned earlier (see note 110), was drawn and quartered and her body parts fed to dogs.

692 The *Mocedades* is correctly thought to be a fictional account of Rodrigo's youth. But this episode of a single combat against Don Martín González, a champion warrior from Navarre, finds a parallel in the brief narration of Rodrigo's youth in the *Historia Roderici*, generally considered by historians to be an accurate account of the Castilian's life (chap. 5).

694 Santa Cruz de mayo is traditionally celebrated on 3 May. This festivity commemorates the discovery of the cross of Christ by Saint Helena, mother of the Emperor Constantine. This day was given special attention by Celtic liturgists in the West and has come to be known with the title of 'Invention of the Cross' (*Catholic Encyclopedia*). Its first mention is in the Silos lectionary, a monastery of Burgos, not far from the events of the poem.

695 A line is probably omitted, giving the name of the Moorish attacker from Atienza, later identified as Garay in line 749. The next two lines are garbled, attaching the same name to two other Moorish kings, and failing to say that they had formed an alliance with Christian traitors to attack Castile.

706 Since there is no higher authority to do it, King Fernando will have to dub himself knight in Santiago's cathedral.

713 After just two battles, not five, unless some are omitted by this version, Rodrigo offers to be the king's subject if the king will make himself worthy by knighting himself. Rodrigo never mentioned to the king that Moors were attacking the kingdom. This strategy allows Rodrigo to organize the defence of the kingdom, and to credit it to his scorecard of battles.

719 Rodrigo escorts the king part of the way to Santiago, and then turns back to face the Moorish invasion.

723–26 Rodrigo's father and uncles gather at San Esteban on the Duero to repel the Moorish onslaught. The identification of the uncles and the towns they hold is simple and direct, more in line with the style of the poem than the earlier genealogies.

731 *Al quarto.* This line makes little sense, unless it is connected with line 744, giving it the meaning that the battle lasted three days, they hoped to fight on to the fourth and emerge victorious. It seems likely that this is another instance of the splitting up of passages that were once coherent. Overall the description of the battle is marked by digressions and false starts, including the three lines of consonantal rhyme (vowels and consonants constituting the rhyme) in lines 740–2.

733 The father and uncles all die in this horrible battle.

740–43 To portray Rodrigo as a great fighter, the poet compares him with ancient figures, one biblical and three Greek, a common device in the medieval poetry that had literary pretensions, but unexpected in this more popular work. The names were chosen for their (consonantal) rhyme. The Ptolemy best known today was an astronomer and geographer, but there was also a warrior king by that name.

746 *Esto le aconsejó por el buen rey don Fernando.* This battle represents a turning point in Rodrigo's attitude towards the king. The counts' betrayal compels him to side with the king.

764 *Santa María la Antigua.* A church. A person who sought refuge in a church was supposed to be safe from harm.

766–7 Rodrigo violates sanctuary, breaking into the church and seizing the count. This is a serious transgression, comparable to criminal acts committed by most of the classic folk heroes.

790–803 In this passage Bishop Bernaldo is driven from Palencia and the king is unable to help him. This new threat to the church in Palencia is never resolved in the extant version of the poem, which was left unfinished. Of the three Palencia passages, this one fits the context of the narrative best. It links Palencia and the inadequate young King Fernando, while hinting at a connection with Rodrigo. The narrative then moves in another direction, but Rodrigo may have returned later to settle the score with the sons of Count Don Pedro del Canpó.

799–803 The king looks very weak here indeed. Rodrigo is absent, supposedly he has been exiled from the kingdom, although there is no reference to this in the main narrative.

805–1225 This is the final episode of the poem, the threat to Spanish sovereignty from France and the aggressive armed response by Rodrigo and King Fernando. As explained in the Introduction (The *Mocedades* Narrative), Rodrigo assumes the role of Bernardo del Carpio, the earliest of the Spanish epic heroes, who defeated Charlemagne and killed Roland and the other French nobles celebrated in the *Chanson de Roland.* The story of Bernardo del Carpio is told in vibrant detail in three thirteenth-century chronicles, two fairly divergent Latin versions, and a translation and compilation of these earlier texts in the vernacular chronicle known to scholars today as the *Estoria de España* (ca. 1284). Much like the reference here to the letters received by King Fernando demanding tribute from the king of France, the German emperor, and the Roman pope (ll. 805–7), in the chronicle version King Alfonso II of Asturias receives a letter making him a vassal of Charlemagne, who is referred to as 'Carlos, enperador de los romanos et de los alemanes et rey de los françeses' [Charles, emperor of the Romans and of the Germans and king of the French]. Additional similarities between the two stories include the challenge to Spanish sovereignty from France, the lone response to foreign aggression by the hero, and the successful retaliation against the French in armed combat. Just as Bernardo del Carpio defeated the French at Roncesvalles, in this episode Rodrigo will lead his king and countrymen against the latter-day imperial ambitions of the French.

811–16 When the poem gets really absurd, we start looking for comparable texts elsewhere. A similar demand is made in the 'Old Parts' of *Tristan*, an Old French text that at its beginning also has the earmarks of the heroic initiation tale. The items listed are the nobleman's most prized possessions. The demands are the most humiliating imaginable.

818–23 The king really goes to pieces over this messasge. Once aggressive and successful, here he appears childish and helpless. Rodrigo already appeared as domineering when he advised the king to knight himself. Now he will become even more overbearing.

837–40 Rodrigo now shows a slightly sarcastic streak as he re-interprets the message from abroad. The same message that Fernando read as a threat to Spain's sovereignty, Rodrigo interprets as an invitation to attack and pillage France. Very clever indeed.

844–58 Here the poem begins a litany of the conquests and domains of Fernando I, but this flattery is placed in the midst of an episode in which Rodrigo is compelled to compensate for the inadequacy of King Fernando. This seems to be another instance in which a narrative may have existed independently of the poem and was integrated into the larger *Mocedades* narrative with little concern or awareness of the resulting incoherence. Note, for example, that Fernando is here credited with invading France (ll. 855–8), yet the invasion is about to take place.

These deeds by King Fernando represent a full life and earned him a respected place in history. But the Fernando of Rodrigo's *mocedades* is also a youth, and has not yet accomplished any of the feats described in this passage. In fact, Rodrigo Díaz would have barely begun his career at the time of Fernando's death in 1065, at an advanced age.

This section is in the ó assonance, beginning with *emperador* and continuing with many impressive words: *León, Aragón, señor, mejor*, etc.

848 *Jenzor.* A word borrowed from Old French epic.

851 *E corrió a Sevilla tres vezes en una sazón.* The Alfonsine history *Crónica de veinte reyes* (bk. 8, chap. 8, p. 170) relates how Fernando had caused so much destruction in a summer of raids through Andalusia that Abenhabet, king of Cordoba and Seville, approached him bearing bountiful riches and begging him to end the destruction of his kingdom. In addition to the riches he bore, Abenhabet offered himself as vassal to Fernando and promised to pay tribute every year. Fernando's vassals urged him to accept the offer on the condition that Abenhabet turn over the remains of Saint Justa of Seville, later substituted for the remains of Saint Isidore.

853 *Sant Isidro* or St Isidoro de Sevilla (ca. 568–636). The leading scholar and churchman of Spain's Visigothic period, before the Moorish invasions. He was archbishop of Seville and was buried in the cathedral there. King Fernando, while he held Seville, moved the body to a new tomb in the cathedral of León, as a symbol of his power and the continuity of Leonese rule with that of the Visigoths. A rich description of the discovery and transfer of the saint's remains is offered in the *Historia silense* (chaps. 96–102).

855 This invasion of France is wholly imaginary, in fact preposterous. Yet this entire episode is included in the post-Alfonsine *Crónica de Castilla* (chap. 19) and the Portuguese history of Spain (and Portugal), *Crónica Geral de Espanha de 1344* (vol. 3, chaps. 463–4), both of which are considered expansions of the Alfonsine chronicles, financed and encouraged by the royal courts in Spain and Portugal. In both works the story is presented as historical fact.

859–74 The names include those of a number of the counts who plotted against the king earlier, including Simón Sánchez de Bureba, who was previously called Jimeno Sánchez (l. 761), and who was sentenced to be executed (ll. 784–89), also an uncle of Rodrigo, Galín Laínez, although all four sons of Laín Calvo were killed in the battle against the traitorous counts (l. 733). Others are a '*Crespo de Grañón,*' who in the *Mio Cid* is the archvillain Garci Ordóñez, and a Frenchman, Almerique de Narbonne.

876 Spain 'beyond the Duero' was in Moorish hands until subsequent conquests by Fernando. To note all the apparent geographic errors or inconsistencies in the poem would be unproductive, but this instance is extreme.

894 The Ruédano, or Rhone, runs from Switzerland south to the Mediterranean in eastern and southeastern France, far from any route from Spain to Paris and impossible to cross except by one or two bridges along its length. The author simply picks a French name he happens to remember.

896–909 Suddenly the tone changes as Fernando makes his *arenga*, the call for heroic endeavour that customarily preceded an attack. The words are traditional, borrowed from earlier sources, and copied with errors, but still this passage remains among the most powerful in early literature. It is admirably organized: the declaration of eagerness for the fray (l. 900), the crafty praise of his men and call for their loyalty (ll. 901–3), the cleverly modest expression of humility combined with determination (ll. 904–6), the impending decline of Spain (l. 907), and the judgment of future generations (ll. 908–9). An ordered, complete series of persuasive points, all in simple, direct, but eloquent language – a rare combination in any period.

910 The poet's borrowing was out of place. A lack of response leaves it hanging grotesquely.

933 Garbled line. Probably he used the sword-point to slice up the cloth.

939 *Pero Mudo.* Pero Bermúdez, who was also the standard-bearer in the *Mio Cid.* Here some new details from folklore are attached to him.

950 *Traidor provado.* An affectionate insult, like English 'you rat.'

970 *Latinos.* Savoy, in the eastern and southeastern part of France, was an independent duchy, not part of that country until much later. The author associates it with Italy, so he calls the inhabitants 'Latins.'

970–9 The irony here is uncharacteristic of the poem, suggesting a late origin in contrast with Fernando's harangue, honed by long tradition. The contrast brings out the patchwork character of the work. The sarcasm is sharpened by Rodrigo's false claim that he comes from a humble family. It would be a grave dishonour for a count to fight against a commoner, and even worse to be defeated by him.

980 The count understands the insult and is furious.

987–93 A powerful evocation of the battle fray, from the same traditional source as two passages in the *Mio Cid.* Compare, in the same assonance, *'Veriedes tantas lanças premer e alçar'* (*Cid*, l. 726, also 3615 and following).

1003 *O eres.* Shift to the *tú* form.

1019 *Mercado.* Still sticking to his offensive merchant metaphor.

1039 *Por sí.* In exchange for himself, that is, his freedom.

1045 *¡Enbarraganad a Françia!* The count has offered his daughter in marriage; Rodrigo has implied that his king will marry her, but now, in speaking with the king, proposes that he take her as a concubine instead, in a symbolic humiliation of France. This might be considered justifiable in light of the demands of tribute originally made by the Europeans. Again, this treacherous and dishonourable treatment of the young woman may be accounted for as an aspect of the traditional hero, whose admirable but tragic career in most cases includes mistreatment of defenceless young women.

1059 The change in name implies a change in rank as Rodrigo becomes captain of nine hundred knights.

1090 *Bavieca.* The great warhorse of the hero's mature years. Here the name was added in the margin by a hand of a later time, as is seen by the different style of handwriting and by the break in assonance. The text has accumulated an undetermined number of intended improvements by people who inserted them paying no attention to whether or not they fit the story, the metre, or the rhyme.

1095 *Quando él llegasse.* When the king arrives.

1103 *Doze Pares.* The twelve peers, a literary recollection of a group of supporters of Charlemagne, nearly three centuries before the supposed action of this poem. This mention brings to mind the venerable French epic poem, the *Song of Roland,* which was well known in Spain. In fact, the first written evidence of the narrative is a brief mention in Latin included in a Spanish manuscript. Known as the *Nota Emilianense,* the manuscript is dated between 1065 and 1075, prior to the earliest manuscript version of the French classic (Alonso 1954, 94). The protagonists of the French epic live on in the folk ballad tradition that flourishes in later centuries, and survives well into the twentieth century. The invasion of France and the humiliation of these Frenchmen by a young Rodrigo and King Fernando must have been a source of great satisfaction to a Spanish audience long familiar with the tales of French warriors like Roland.

1135 The pope, apparently frightened by Spain's military might or by Rodrigo's demeanour, talks his allies into proposing a postponement of the impending battle.

1143 Rodrigo is distrustful of the pope, as he was of the king at the court in Zamora. His domination of Fernando, which has grown steadily, now becomes overwhelming, and degrading to the king. The author's concept of heroism, as seen in Rodrigo, and of royalty as well, is really strange, especially for the early fourteenth century, when this late version of the tale was made.

1145 *Muy leídos.* The poet can gain audience approval by playing up to the distrust of writing and writers that is common among illiterate and semi-literate people.

1147 The sight of Rodrigo seems to make the pope fearful, recalling the reaction of the king and the assembly in Zamora, when the youth appeared in all his fury.

1150 The elaborate honours extended to King Fernando and Rodrigo. Are they given out of fear, or the result of the duplicity Rodrigo had warned of?

1161–2 Once the pope knows which Spaniard is the king and which is Rodrigo, he directs himself to the king and creates a new title for him, emperor of Spain. Rodrigo asserts that the five kingdoms of Spain already pay him homage, making him the equal of any emperor.

1164 *Malas graçias.* An impertinent retort, and an unthinkable failure of diplomacy toward the Holy Father.

1166 *Sin vós*. Without your support or intervention.

1167 Several Spanish kings have wanted to be named holy Roman emperor. Only Charles V, a grandson of Ferdinand and Isabel born in Austria, attained that distinction (1519–58).

1172 King Fernando has other ideas. But for now Rodrigo will prevail.

1184 *Alegre se va*. Why, when he wanted a truce? Apparently because of his complete confidence in Rodrigo's ability to win the battle.

1197 *La una e las dos*. Perhaps the attack was to be launched at the count of three.

1198–1200 A miraculous birth? The defeat of the count of Savoy, and the delivery of his daughter to the king, cannot have been more than a few weeks earlier.

1201 The pope must have a spy in the enemy camp. At any rate he seizes the opportunity to baptize the child and create a quasi-family link between Fernando (without his knowledge) and his own allies. So the clash of armies is averted.

1210 Does the pope believe the birth is a miracle, or is he manipulating? And what is the author's intention in making this bizarre invention?

1214–15 Rodrigo demands a surrender, not a truce.

1218–25 If the holy Roman emperor dies before the surrender is completed, Fernando will succeed him. So Fernando is happy to lengthen the delay for sixteen years or more. Rodrigo was right: the hoped-for war is getting bogged down in politics. And if the poem has enough coherence to link his attempted humiliation of France by means of the count's daughter with the birth of the child, then his thirst for killing is now thwarted by his own earlier action. So the ambivalence toward the hero – as a necessary but dangerous figure in society, which is usually seen in the ancient versions of the heroic myth – is reaffirmed by this poem. The poem trails off unfinished at this point, where it seems that Rodrigo has no more role to play until he gets back to Spain to find more warlike enemies. Traditional texts have nothing more to say about him until, in a lost epic now known only through a prose version recorded by historians, and called the *Cantar del Cerco de Zamora* (Song of the Siege of Zamora), he gets involved, while still young, in the fratricidal wars among the heirs of King Fernando. There his role is marked by a serious failure, the only one recorded for him in popular literature, adding a dimension to his heroic character and foreshadowing the exemplary figure of the *Mio Cid*.

In the aftermath of the *Mocedades*, tradition does record one item. The grandson of the count of Savoy, who, being born out of wedlock, could not be heir to king Fernando, lived to become a distinguished and widely admired dignitary of the church.

LINE NUMBERS
FROM EDITIONS OF THE
MOCEDADES DE RODRIGO

This table compares the line numbers from the present edition of the *Mocedades de Rodrigo* with editions of the *Refundición de las Mocedades de Rodrigo* (Funes 2004, 1–117), the *Mocedades de Rodrigo* (Alfonso Pinto 1999, 189–216), and the *Rodrigo y el rey Fernando* (Menéndez Pidal 1980, 257–89). Only the present edition numbers the lines from the first folio of the manuscript, so they will not be listed here. All other editions coincide in the numbering of the first line of the poem – reason enough to use it as a starting point, followed by line 50 from the present edition and every five lines thereafter.

Mocedades de Rodrigo	Funes	Alfonso Pinto	Menéndez Pidal
48	1	1	1
50	3	3	3
55	8	8	8
60	12	12	12
65	17	17	17
70	20	22	21
75	24	26	25
80	29	31	30
85	34	36	35
90	37	41	40
95	44	47	45
100	49	52	50
105	54	57	55
110	59	62	60
115	64	67	65
120	69	72	70

Mocedades de Rodrigo	Funes	Alfonso Pinto	Menéndez Pidal
125	74	77	75
130	79	82	80
135	84	87	85
140	89	92	90
145	94	97	94
150	99	102	99
155	104	107	104
160	109	112	109
165	114	117	114
170	119	122	119
175	124	128	124
180	129	133	129
185	134	137	134
190	139	142	139
195	143	147	144
200	148	152	149
205	153	157	154
210	158	162	159
215	163	167	164
220	168	172	169
225	173	177	174
230	178	182	179
235	183	187	184
240	188	192	190
245	193	197	195
250	198	202	200
255	203	207	205
260	208	212	210
265	213	217	215
270	218	222	220
275	223	227	225
280	228	232	230
285	233	237	235
290	238	242	240
295	243	247	245
300	249	252	251
305	–	257	255
310	–	262	259
315	250	266	263
320	255	271	268

Mocedades de Rodrigo	Funes	Alfonso Pinto	Menéndez Pidal
325	260	276	273
330	265	281	278
335	270	286	283
340	274	290	287
345	279	295	292
350	284	300	297
355	289	305	302
360	294	310	307
365	299	315	312
370	303	319	316
375	308	324	321
380	313	329	326
385	318	333	331
390	322	338	336
395	327	343	341
400	332	348	346
405	337	353	351
410	342	358	356
415	347	363	361
420	352	368	366
425	357	373	371
430	362	378	376
435	367	383	381
440	372	388	386
445	377	393	391
450	382	398	396
455	387	403	401
460	392	408	406
465	397	413	411
470	402	418	416
475	407	423	421
480	412	428	426
485	417	433	431
490	422	438	436
495	427	443	441
500	432	448	446
505	437	453	451
510	442	458	456
515	447	463	461
520	452	468	466

Mocedades de Rodrigo	Funes	Alfonso Pinto	Menéndez Pidal
525	457	473	471
530	462	478	476
535	466	483	480
540	472	488	485
545	477	493	490
550	482	498	495
555	487	503	500
560	492	508	505
565	497	513	510
570	502	518	515
575	507	523	520
580	512	528	525
585	517	533	530
590	522	538	535
595	527	543	540
600	532	548	545
605	537	553	550
610	542	558	555
615	547	563	560
620	552	568	565
625	557	573	570
630	561	578	575
635	566	583	580
640	571	588	585
645	576	593	590
650	581	598	595
655	586	603	600
660	589	607	603
665	595	613	609
670	600	618	614
675	605	623	619
680	610	628	624
685	615	633	629
690	620	638	634
695	625	643	639
700	630	648	644
705	635	653	649
710	639	657	653
715	644	662	658
720	649	667	663

Mocedades de Rodrigo	Funes	Alfonso Pinto	Menéndez Pidal
725	654	672	668
730	659	677	673
735	664	682	678
740	669	687	683
745	674	692	688
750	678	696	692
755	683	701	697
760	688	706	702
765	693	711	707
770	698	716	712
775	703	721	717
780	708	726	722
785	713	731	727
790	718	736	732
795	723	741	737
800	728	746	742
805	733	751	747
810	738	756	752
815	743	760	757
820	748	764	762
825	753	769	767
830	758	774	772
835	763	779	777
840	768	784	782
845	774	789	787
850	779	794	792
855	784	799	797
860	789	804	802
865	–	809	807
870	798	814	812
875	803	819	817
880	808	824	822
885	813	829	827
890	818	834	832
895	823	839	837
900	828	844	843
905	832	849	847
910	837	854	852
915	842	859	857
920	847	864	862

Mocedades de Rodrigo	Funes	Alfonso Pinto	Menéndez Pidal
925	852	869	867
930	857	874	872
935	862	879	877
940	866	883	881
945	871	888	886
950	876	893	891
955	881	898	896
960	886	902	901
965	891	907	906
970	896	912	911
975	901	917	916
980	906	922	921
985	911	927	926
990	916	932	931
995	921	937	936
1000	926	942	941
1005	931	947	946
1010	936	952	951
1015	941	958	956
1020	947	963	962
1025	952	968	967
1030	957	973	972
1035	962	978	977
1040	967	983	982
1045	972	988	987
1050	977	993	992
1055	983	998	997
1060	987	1003	1002
1065	992	1008	1007
1070	996	1013	1011
1075	1000	1017	1015
1080	1005	1022	1020
1085	1010	1027	1025
1090	1015	1032	1030
1095	1020	1037	1035
1100	1025	1042	1040
1105	1030	1047	1045
1110	1035	1052	1050
1115	1040	1057	1055
1120	1045	1062	1060

Mocedades de Rodrigo	Funes	Alfonso Pinto	Menéndez Pidal
1125	1050	1067	1065
1130	1055	1072	1070
1135	1060	1077	1075
1140	1066	1082	1081
1145	1071	1087	1086
1150	1076	1092	1091
1155	1081	1097	1096
1160	1086	1102	1101
1165	1091	1107	1106
1170	1096	1112	1111
1175	1101	1117	1116
1180	1106	1122	1120
1185	1111	1127	1125
1190	1116	1132	1130
1195	1121	1137	1135
1200	1126	1142	1140
1205	1131	1147	1145
1210	1136	1152	1150
1215	1141	1157	1155
1220	1145	1162	1159
1225	1150	1167	1164

INDEX